P9-AFM-658

DOOMSDAY

Herbert Windolf
625 Angelita Dr.
Prescott, AZ 86303-5014

DOOMSDAY

End-of-the-World Scenarios

Richard Moran

ALPHA

A Pearson Education Company

For my wife, Annie—my love, my partner, my soul mate, my "bestest buddy"

Copyright © 2003 by Richard Moran

All rights reserved. No part of this book shall be reproduced, stored in a retrieval system, or transmitted by any means, electronic, mechanical, photocopying, recording, or otherwise, without written permission from the publisher. No patent liability is assumed with respect to the use of the information contained herein. Although every precaution has been taken in the preparation of this book, the publisher and author assume no responsibility for errors or omissions. Neither is any liability assumed for damages resulting from the use of information contained herein. For information, address Alpha Books, 201 West 103rd Street, Indianapolis, IN 46290.

International Standard Book Number: 0-02-864315-1
Library of Congress Catalog Card Number: 2002111664

04 03 02   8 7 6 5 4 3 2 1

Interpretation of the printing code: The rightmost number of the first series of numbers is the year of the book's printing; the rightmost number of the second series of numbers is the number of the book's printing. For example, a printing code of 02-1 shows that the first printing occurred in 2002.

Printed in the United States of America

Note: This publication contains the opinions and ideas of its author. It is intended to provide helpful and informative material on the subject matter covered. It is sold with the understanding that the author and publisher are not engaged in rendering professional services in the book. If the reader requires personal assistance or advice, a competent professional should be consulted.

The author and publisher specifically disclaim any responsibility for any liability, loss, or risk, personal or otherwise, which is incurred as a consequence, directly or indirectly, of the use and application of any of the contents of this book.

Trademarks: All terms mentioned in this book that are known to be or are suspected of being trademarks or service marks have been appropriately capitalized. Alpha Books and Pearson Education, Inc., cannot attest to the accuracy of this information. Use of a term in this book should not be regarded as affecting the validity of any trademark or service mark.

For marketing and publicity, please call: 317-581-3722

The publisher offers discounts on this book when ordered in quantity for bulk purchases and special sales.

For sales within the United States, please contact: Corporate and Government Sales, 1-800-382-3419 or corpsales@pearsontechgroup.com

Outside the United States, please contact: International Sales, 317-581-3793 or international@pearsontechgroup.com

CONTENTS

PROLOGUE

The cataclysmic events I describe in *DOOMSDAY* are not meant to frighten readers but to forewarn. Each scenario is based on thoroughly researched science. The terrifying threats posed by both man and nature that you will read about in this book could all actually happen. And when one of these episodes inevitably does occur, it may well wipe out all life on earth.

Following completion of *DOOMSDAY*, a score of news stories came out attesting to the reality of the 10 stark scenarios I have presented.

Chapter 1 examines the threat that terrorists or a rogue nation would attack the United States or our allies with weapons of mass destruction. As I write these words, President Bush is rallying the nation for a possible preemptive strike against Iraq to depose Saddam Hussein and eliminate the threat that he will use chemical, biological, or nuclear weapons against us, perhaps killing millions of Americans.

Chapter 2 explores the possibility that an asteroid could someday impact earth, bringing about the mass extinction of every living species on the planet. In July 2002, the BBC released a startling story that a newly discovered asteroid scientists have named 2002 NT7 may indeed bc on a direct trajectory for the earth and could strike the planet in February 2019. Although most astronomers now believe that the asteroid will narrowly miss the earth, not all agree, and it has been classified as the most dangerous Near Earth Object ever detected.

Chapter 5 presents evidence that the greenhouse effect is causing global warming that may lead to myriad catastrophic consequences, including the melting of the polar ice sheets followed by a sea level rise that could inundate such coastal cities as New York and Los Angeles. In July 2002, CNN published an article reporting that, "Scientists have long warned that global warming—when heat-trapping gases force atmospheric temperatures to rise—could eventually raise sea levels to a dangerous point by melting ice sheets and glaciers."

Chapter 7 delves into the possibility that future plagues could have a catastrophic impact on the human species. Through the summer of 2002, almost every media source in the United States ran stories about this year's deadly outbreak of West Nile Virus, a disease that first appeared here in 1999. The virus will—in all probability—claim fewer than 1,000 lives this year. But how many will die next year? How many five years from now? This is a virus Americans have never been exposed to before, and we have no immunity to the disease. Could West Nile Virus turn into the most virulent virus ever to strike our country, perhaps taking millions of lives? No one yet knows.

Chapter 10 reports on bioengineering blunders. In 2001, the Union of Concerned Scientists issued a fact sheet warning that, "In addition to posing risks of harm that we can envision and attempt to assess, genetic engineering may also pose risks that we simply do not know enough [about] to identify."

As you will discover in these pages, our existence as the dominant species on earth is not assured. Indeed, the odds are that humankind is already doomed.

ACKNOWLEDGMENTS

I would first like to thank Gary Goldstein and Phil Kitchel for their invaluable editorial suggestions and insight during the writing of this book.

I am also indebted to my literary agent, John Talbot, whose astute representation has served both my work and myself so ably over the past year.

Finally, I wish to thank my very dear friends Glenna and Del Goulet, whose encouragement and support during the writing of *DOOMSDAY* helped me climb many a literary hill.

Richard Moran

WEAPONS OF MASS DESTRUCTION

Of all the dangers threatening humanity's continued existence on Earth, the greatest and most immediate is humanity itself. Less than a million years ago, an upright primate with monkey curiosity and opposable thumbs—our illustrious ancestor—began to assert its primacy and dominion over all living things on the planet. Now, Homo sapiens are at the top of the food chain, the dominant species.

But while the human race's diabolical ingenuity at conceiving new ways to kill its fellows is unparalleled, its moral development and judgment—in a word, wisdom—has lagged far behind the progress of its inventions.

More than half a century ago in WWII, atomic sunfire was unleashed on Hiroshima and Nagasaki, creating a literal hell on Earth. In the almost 60 years since, no atomic bombs have been used in war, and so we have forgotten the awesome destructiveness of the weapons we have created. Worse, the ability and technology needed to create the unholy trinity of nuclear, biological, and chemical weapons has filtered down to several dozen nations of widely differing character and aspirations.

In the summer of 1914, a conflict in the Balkans quickly widened into the First World War. Now, the region of Kashmir has become the world's number-one hotspot. Located in a vast mountain valley between the borders of Pakistan and India, which have contended bitterly for its ownership since they both declared themselves as countries in 1947, Kashmir is a lush, scenic, troubled region. Part of it belongs to Pakistan, part to India, with a well-fortified borderline of demarcation between the two. Pakistan is an Islamic country, while India is predominantly Hindu. The majority of Kashmiris are Islamic, including those ruled by Hindu India.

Pakistan and India have warred three times in the past over Kashmir, with India victorious every time. But at the close of the twentieth century, a new and deadly factor entered the picture, as Pakistan successfully developed an atomic bomb. This was the long-awaited "Islamic Bomb," the first nuclear weapon developed by an Islamist country, long a goal of Iran, Iraq, and other countries in the region. The hated Zionist foe in Israel had possessed atomic bombs since the mid-1960s, though refusing to acknowledge the fact. Now Islamic self-esteem could pride itself in possessing a weapon of mass destruction that would counter that of the Israelis—and any other potential interloper in the region.

CHAPTER 1: WEAPONS OF MASS DESTRUCTION

With a population of more than 150 million, Pakistan was ruled by a military dictatorship with strong links to radical, anti-Western Muslim fundamentalists. The military spy and secret police system, the ISI, was instrumental in installing the Taliban regime in Afghanistan. Thousands of members of al Qaeda, the terror corps led by Osama bin Laden, had been allowed to cross the border from Afghanistan into Pakistan, where they now sheltered and prospered. Bin Laden himself was rumored to be hiding in Pakistan.

Pakistan had long sponsored terrorist groups aimed at destabilizing India's control of Kashmir. The groups had their training camps and bases in Pakistan, while sending units across the border to commit acts of sabotage and assassination in Kashmir. Their bloody deeds done, the terrorists would slip back across the border into Pakistan, safe from pursuing Indian troops.

Heartened by the United States's policy, which stated that regimes that harbored and sponsored terrorism were themselves guilty of terrorism, India prepared to take strong military action to suppress Pakistani-backed violence in Kashmir. A multi-ethnic state and the world's largest democracy, India's million-person army outnumbered Pakistan's by a factor of three to one. Having long had the atomic bomb, India had stockpiled an arsenal of about 100 such weapons. Pakistan, rushing their weapon into production, had managed to build about 25 nuclear weapons. Both nations possessed short-range missiles (with a reach of several hundred miles) and long range missiles (with a reach of 1,000 to 1,500 miles). This put the capitals of both states within each other's reach.

A series of particularly garish, Pakistan-backed atrocities against Indian troops in Kashmir and a failed attempt to massacre the Indian Parliament in New Delhi had convinced India's leaders of the necessity to make war on Pakistan. Almost 300,000 Indian troops were massed along the Kashmir-Pakistan border, while on the other side of the line stood about 225,000 Pakistani troops.

The attempts of peacemakers to broker a stand-down between the two countries failed. Unfortunately, the efforts of troublemakers were more successful, with al Qaeda members in particular striving to ignite a holy war, this time not against the godless West, but against Hindu India. A massacre of several Kashmiri villages friendly to the Indian cause was taken by the government in New Delhi as *casus belli*—an act of war.

Indian troops thrust across the border into Pakistan, encountering fierce resistance from the defenders. Titanic clashes between massive armies, tank battalions, and artillery batteries resulted in thousands of deaths and tens of thousands of casualties on both sides. Like all "holy wars," it was prosecuted with bitter ferocity by both combatants. But the Indian army's superior hardware and resources were the deciding factor. Despite fight-to-the-last-soldier resistance, Pakistani troops were being pushed back, their defensive line in danger of giving way to the invaders.

Until now, it had been a war waged with conventional weapons, though no less lethal. Now, with the Indian army poised to make a breakthrough that would open the road to Islamabad, the Pakistani high command made a grave decision to use their last resort: atomic weapons.

Zero Hour. Buttons were pushed, launching salvoes of atomic missiles at India. Pakistan's nuclear attack was two-pronged, delivering the weapons by fighter-bomber jets and guided missiles. Squadrons of fighter-bomber jets, escorted by fighter-interceptors, arrowed toward the Indian capital. The invading Indian troops on the front lines were not targeted, for fear of killing Pakistani defenders and radioactively contaminating homeland soil. Instead, short-range missiles were aimed at Indian supply bases in Kashmir. A mixed sortie of fighter-bombers and long-range missiles were aimed at New Delhi and Bombay. Pakistani jet pilots were well trained. One of them managed to get though to deliver an atomic bomb on New Delhi, obliterating it.

Pakistani High Command had underestimated the power of the atom. Their salvo of rockets hammered Kashmir, obscuring it between the writhing mushroom clouds that rose from the first atomic attack in more than 50 years. The vale of Kashmir was pulverized, cratered, riven, seared, and poisoned with lethal radioactive fallout, killing millions.

The moment that Indian radarscope technicians first detected the launch of Pakistani missiles, the signal was given to fire India's own atomic counterstrike. An Indian missile hit Islamabad, erasing it, a mushroom cloud rising over fragmented rubble that only an instant before had been a populous city.

CHAPTER 1: WEAPONS OF MASS DESTRUCTION

Prepared for Indian counterstrikes, Pakistani High Command had established a number of command posts in secure sites, far from the cities. As Kandahar was incinerated by Indian atomic fire, a Pakistani general ordered commencement of Operation Sayaf al Islam—Sword of Islam. Islamist fanatics in the military and their al Qaeda allies had vowed that, though Pakistan be destroyed in atomic conflict with India, the Great Satan USA and its Zionist allies would not escape unscathed.

A long-range guided missile, more powerful and sophisticated than any other in the Pakistani missile arsenal, had been procured, armed with an atomic warhead, and targeted at Tel Aviv in Israel. The go-signal was given, and the Sword of Islam lofted skyward, arcing not eastward, toward India, but westward, toward the Middle East.

The missile fell short of its goal, impacting not in Israel, but in Jordan. At this time, preparing for a unilateral regime change in Iraq, the United States had nearly completed a massive 200,000-troop buildup in Jordan, poised to take the overland route into Iraq the moment Washington gave the order to attack. Jordan hadn't wanted to cooperate, but arm-twisting by top U.S. administration officials had convinced them to allow their country to be used as a staging area for the invasion of Iraq.

Now the Sword of Islam missile detonated—several scores of miles from where U.S. troops were assembled, but too close. In Washington, confused initial reports indicated that the missile had been fired not by Pakistan (heretofore considered an "ally"), but rather by Iraq. It appeared as though the Iraqi dictator had managed to procure and launch an atomic missile. The White House ordered a nuclear strike against Baghdad.

In the meantime, the Iraqis, themselves in the dark about the Pakistani launch, assumed that the atomic bomb had been exploded by the Americans, preparatory to launching an all-out attack. The Iraqis had no atomic weapons, but possessed in abundance the "poor man's nukes": chemical and biological weapons. SCUD missiles armed with warheads filled with anthrax and poison gas were fired from Iraq, arcing toward their targets at the U.S. invasion force staging area and in Israel.

Not to be caught napping, the Israelis had already launched a fusillade of nuclear missiles at Iraq. Then Iran got into the act.

The world's first—and possibly last—nuclear/biological war had begun.

■

On the morning of September 11, 2001, 3,465 men, women, and children in New York, Washington, and Pennsylvania were murdered by fanatical Islamic fundamentalists, and life in America was radically changed. Our peace of mind was shattered, replaced by a fear and foreboding that swept our land. It was suddenly no longer safe to fly, no longer safe to work in a skyscraper, no longer just a job to be an American soldier, sailor, or airman.

During World War I, World War II, Korea, Vietnam, and the Persian Gulf War, our homeland, protected by vast oceans and airspace, had seemed invulnerable to the carnage and horror of the wars that raged in Europe, Asia, and the Middle East. The wholesale death that has through history been part and parcel of the incessant wars between nations, ethnic groups, and ideologies could not reach us here. Then came that terrible fall day—the Pearl Harbor of the third millennia—when a handful of terrorists turned our airliners into guided missiles and all of us awoke to the realization that our security was no more tangible than the soot that billowed above the burning World Trade Center.

The memories of that terrible day are still too raw for any of us to need a reminder of what happened, and where the attacks on our country have led us. We are at war in Afghanistan, and future battles loom in Iraq, Yemen, Somalia, Indonesia, and the Philippines. Yet our young warriors in uniform will for the most part face conventional weapons in which they've been highly trained. No small number will forever lie in the hallowed ground of military cemeteries, but most of our boys will come back.

Can we be as sure that we shall not face far more catastrophic casualties here at home in the tumultuous years that lie ahead as hatred of American policies becomes ever more virulent abroad? Evidence has mounted since the September 11 attacks that Osama bin Laden and his fanatical followers have actively been trying to acquire nuclear, biological, and chemical weapons for some time, and that they may now possess one or more of these weapons of mass destruction. Intelligence experts are certain that the terrorists intend to use these weapons against America.

NO SAFE PLACE

Safety at home is no longer our birthright. Somewhere out there, terrorists and outlaw nations are at this very moment planning chemical, biological, radiological, or nuclear attacks—all classified as weapons of mass destruction (WMD)—on large urban areas of the United States, Europe, Japan, and other countries. Such attacks could kill tens of thousands of people—or even millions if a nuclear weapons is used—in one fell swoop.

Lethal chemical, biological, or radiological agents could be spread over cities by terrorists or operatives from rogue nations dropping the toxins from small private planes, or simply releasing the agents from plastic containers. While hazardous materials teams would undoubtedly be rushed to the contaminated area and victims would be treated with Cipro and other curative drugs, fatalities would undoubtedly still be high, especially among the very young, the very old, and those with existing health problems. Long-term debilitating illnesses would also be widespread in the affected area following such an attack.

If terrorists succeeded in smuggling a nuclear device into the United States and detonating it in the middle of a large city like New York or Chicago, the death toll would far exceed the fatalities caused by a chemical, biological, or radiological attack. It is a disturbing fact that some modern nuclear bombs are as small as an ordinary suitcase and can be easily transported anywhere.

Although everyone is aware of the deadly potential of nuclear bombs, few know the difference between chemical, biological, and radiological weapons. Essentially, chemical agents can be broken down into two classes: nerve agents that attack the nervous system and surface agents that penetrate the body through inhalation or skin contact.

> Some modern nuclear bombs are as small as an ordinary suitcase and can be easily transported anywhere.

Nerve agents act by blocking the transmission of nerve messages through the disruption of a neurotransmitter called acetylcholine. Nerve agents include Sarin, Soman, Tabun, and VX, all of which can cause death within minutes. Surface agents, which include phosgene, chlorine, hydrogen cyanide, and mustard gases, can cause death by causing the lungs to fill with water, destroying the respiratory tract, or blocking oxygen from entering the blood stream. Mustard gas is a blistering agent that can damage the skin, eyes, and lungs.

Biological agents used to kill humans include viruses, bacteria, fungi, and other poisonous microorganisms. Today, there is a significant and growing danger that terrorists will unleash lethal amounts of anthrax, bubonic plague bacteria, smallpox virus, or some other biological agent over densely populated areas such as New York, Chicago, Los Angeles, Tokyo, London, or Paris. If terrorists should succeed in bioengineering one or more of these organisms—creating mutant strains that are even more deadly than the original agent—the danger that biological weapons pose will increase dramatically.

What makes biological agents especially insidious is that they can reproduce. Thus, if a biological agent is not brought under control quickly, the disease-causing bacteria or virus can spread rapidly, causing ever-increasing fatalities.

Although not a living agent, botulism toxin is yet another lethal biological weapon. If only a relatively small amount of the toxin were simultaneously introduced into the water systems of the largest American cities at some point after the water has been purified by treatment plants—for instance, if terrorists gained access to the main supply pipes running from the plants to the homes of consumers—hundreds of thousands of people could be poisoned before authorities realized what was happening. While antibiotics would be effective in treating the existing form of botulism, if terrorists succeeded in developing a deadlier form of the toxin—a very real possibility in this age of increasingly sophisticated biotechnology—countless people could perish before a new antibiotic was found.

Radiological weapons include plutonium, fission products, spent fuel from civilian reactors, and artificially produced radioactive materials. If terrorists or rogue nations such as Iraq were to spread a radiological weapon over a densely populated area, millions would die, and the land would be contaminated and uninhabitable for eons to come.

Intelligence sources in the United States, Europe, and Asia—including the CIA, the British MI6 Secret Intelligence Service, the Israeli Mossad, the Russian KGB, and the Japanese Defense Intelligence Headquarters—have little doubt that a frightening number of extremists and several rogue nations are trying to obtain chemical, biological, and radiological weapons, and perhaps nuclear devices as well. Because of the increasingly porous borders between countries, both terrorists and outlaw nations have the ability to strike anywhere in the modern world.

CHEMICAL TERROR

This Armageddon of WMD has already begun. During the morning rush hour on Monday, March 19, 1995, a chemical hell engulfed the Tokyo subway system. As hundreds of thousands of Japanese commuters were riding to work, terrorists released canisters of the deadly nerve gas Sarin in several crowded trains.

First formulated by the Nazis during World War II, Sarin is colorless, odorless, and 26 times more deadly than cyanide gas. A single pinprick-size droplet will inflict an agonizing death on a human being within minutes. Sarin attacks the nerve endings of the body, causing eye pain and blurred vision, convulsions, tightness in the chest, excessive salivation and sweating, and nausea and vomiting. The agent also invades the gastrointestinal tract and bladder, forcing people to involuntarily defecate and urinate in their clothing. The greatest danger to human life comes when Sarin enters the upper respiratory tract. People first experience a constriction of the muscles in their chests, and then bronchospasms begin, followed soon afterwards by respiratory failure and death.

As the Sarin gas spread through the crowded Tokyo subway system that nightmarish Monday morning, thousands could suddenly barely see or breathe, and began vomiting and defecating uncontrollably. Many experienced irregular cardiac rhythm that brought them to the brink of a heart attack.

There is no question that Sarin was used in the terrorist attack on the Tokyo subway system. Yet according to Clark Staten, executive director of the Emergency Response and Research Institute (ERRI) in

Chicago, Sarin is such an extremely toxic substance that it "should have killed hundreds or thousands."

Staten suspects that either the Sarin was chemically different than the pure nerve agent stockpiled by the military, or that the terrorists employed a combination of Sarin and other nerve agents in a sinister plot to confuse responding police, fire department, and emergency medical services.

Whether the terrorists used Sarin alone or a mixture of nerve agents, the demonic attack produced a scene out of Dante's *Inferno*. A tidal wave of screams and cries for help swept through the stations as pandemonium seized the subway passengers. Thousands streamed toward the exits, fighting and clawing their way through the narrow gates. Hundreds were trampled or crushed against walls and entryways.

The final human toll was 12 dead and 5,500 injured. However, it was not only the subway riders gassed by the deadly Sarin who suffered, but the entire Japanese people. Fear gripped the country as word of the terrorist attack spread. If a deadly nerve gas could be released in the Tokyo subway system, it could be used to poison people in literally any public place. The nerve agent could conceivably be spread through office or apartment buildings, or fill the air of quiet residential areas with its lethal vapors. The deadly Sarin attack posed the greatest threat to the Japanese people since the end of World War II, and police and counterterrorist agencies began an intensive search for the terrorists.

Attention soon focused on the extremist religious sect called Aum Shinrikyo (Supreme Truth). Founded in 1984 by "Venerated Master" Shoko Asahara, the cult was suspected of being behind a Sarin gas attack in the central Japanese city of Matsumoto in June 1994, which killed seven people.

As evidence mounted that members of Aum Shinrikyo were responsible, arrest warrants were issued for Shoko Asahara and 200 of his followers. After an intensive manhunt, Asahara was finally captured during a police raid on the Aum headquarters at the base of Mount Fuji.

Asahara and those arrested with him were later tried by a Japanese court, and several senior members of the sect were sentenced to death by hanging for their hideous crimes against innocent people. Many of the cult members who were found guilty are appealing their convictions, and as of the writing of this book in late 2001 their cases are still before Japanese courts.

As diabolical as the Tokyo subway attack was, it was hardly the first time chemical or biological agents have been used to kill human beings. Terrorism expert Brian M. Jenkins has reported that the leaders of Aum Shinrikyo were inspired to release Sarin gas in the Tokyo subway after learning of Iraq's use of chemical weapons during its war with Iran. Incredibly, the use of chemical weapons dates back to the fifth century B.C.E. when ancient armies hurled flaming oil and fireballs called "Greek fire" at their enemies.

A WEAPON OF DISEASE

In the fourteenth century, a hideous new biological weapon was introduced when an army besieging Kaffa, a Russian seaport on the Black Sea, catapulted plague-infected cadavers into the city. In colonial America, a British officer gave smallpox-infected blankets to local Native Americans, hoping to spread the disease among tribes thought to be allied with the French.

During World War I, both the Germans and the Allies employed chlorine and mustard gases to poison opposing troops. The suffering of individual soldiers was so great that it led to the establishment of the 1925 Geneva Protocol, which banned the use of chemical or bacteriological agents in warfare. Most major nations—with the odd exception of the United States—became parties to the agreement, but this did not stop some countries from using chemical and biological warfare in the years to come.

The modern history of biological warfare can be traced back to the Japanese. In 1918, the Japanese army established a special section called Unit 731, dedicated to the development of biological weapons of war. In one of the cruelest acts in history, the poisonous agents were tested on helpless prisoners of war. Then, in 1941, Japanese planes repeatedly sprayed bubonic plague over several areas of China. At the same time, the Japanese released hordes of plague-infested rats. Bubonic plague can be treated effectively today with tetracycline or doxycycline—but the Chinese had neither. The exact death toll among Chinese peasants is unknown to this day, but it surely amounted to hundreds of thousands of innocent civilians perishing in unspeakable pain.

It is possible that somewhere terrorists are breeding rats infected with either the existing form of bubonic plague, or a newly bioengineered strain of the disease that is far more deadly. It would be a simple matter to truck several thousand of these disease-carrying animals into a large city and release them in some dark alley. The plague would soon spread to the millions of other rats infesting most large cities, and then to humans. It is impossible to estimate how many would die. Antidotes to bubonic plague are in scarce supply, and hospitals are ill equipped to handle an outbreak of the disease. If the terrorists released plague-infested rats in New York, London, Paris, Moscow, Tokyo, or any other large city, medical facilities would be overwhelmed, at least in the short term, and unable to treat many of the first to become infected.

Japan is not the only country whose chemical and biological experiments during World War II provide today's terrorists—as well as rogue nations like Iraq, Libya, and North Korea—with insidious and difficult-to-detect weapons to use against civilian populations. During the war, German scientists developed the deadly Sarin nerve agent used in the Tokyo subway attack, and Great Britain conducted extensive research into biological bombs that could disperse lethal anthrax spores over wide areas of enemy territory.

> It would be simple to truck several thousand disease-carrying animals into a large city and release them in some dark alley.

The research was conducted on Gruinard Island off the coast of Scotland. The experiments resulted in the soil of the island being saturated with Bacillus anthracis spores—a biological disaster that made Gruinard uninhabitable to this day—and even spread to herds of cattle and sheep on the nearby coast of Scotland. Conceivably, terrorists wearing protective clothing could land a small boat on Gruinard, collect anthrax spores, and cultivate them in some secret laboratory until they had enough spores to spread the deadly biological agent over entire cities.

Assuming the terrorists dispersed the present form of anthrax, most of those people infected could be treated with Cipro or other drugs and would likely survive. However, if—as in the worst case scenarios involving other biological weapons—the terrorists released a bioengineered strain of anthrax for which we do not yet have a cure, the death toll could be catastrophic.

Is this a fanciful scenario? Hardly. The odds that terrorist groups or some outlaw country will attack the United States, Europe, or Japan with chemical, biological, radiological, or nuclear weapons grows by the day. Tomorrow, next month, next year, some large city will either disintegrate beneath a mushroom cloud or dissolve into chaos; vital infrastructures like communications, transportation, food distribution, banking, and social services will be unable to function as their staffs are decimated by a man-made plague. Because terrorist activities have become increasingly sophisticated, no one on the planet is out of the reach of extremists.

NUCLEAR HORROR

Ironically, the disintegration of the Soviet Union in 1991, which put an end to the Cold War and the threat of nuclear annihilation that had hung over the world for decades, also opened the floodgates for terrorist groups to gain access to WMD. The breakup of the Soviet system into numerous independent countries led to a drastic loosening of government control over weapons of war, including the USSR's nuclear arsenal. Terrorist groups and agents of rogue nations were quick to spot their opportunity. The collapse of the Soviet economy meant that the military went unpaid for months on end. Officers and enlisted people, desperate for money to feed their families, began selling their weapons on the black market.

Pressured to pay off its enormous foreign debt, the Russian government also began selling military equipment, including a fleet of submarines to Iran. At the same time, the breakup of central control in the Soviet Union led to increasingly lax security over the nation's arsenal of chemical, biological, radiological, and nuclear weapons. The Soviet Union is known to have manufactured a large supply of anthrax and other deadly biological weapons, and, in the confusion of Russia and the other former Soviet republics, neither the CIA nor other intelligence services knows if any deadly agents have been stolen and sold to terrorists by poverty-stricken scientists and soldiers.

Equally frightening, intelligence reports gathered within Russia and the other former republics indicate that an unknown number of nuclear weapons are unaccounted for, and may have been secretly sold to rogue nations or terrorist groups. Consider for a moment the implications of this scenario. If, for instance, any of the missing chemical, biological, radiological, or nuclear weapons find their way into the hands of the al Qaeda group, the consequences, especially for the United States and Israel, could be catastrophic.

Osama bin Laden is believed to have at least 3,000 fanatical followers, any number of whom could smuggle deadly nerve gases, anthrax spores, bubonic plague, radiological weapons, or nuclear devices into New York or Tel Aviv. Some of these terrorists would undoubtedly be apprehended before they could employ their deadly weapons. But it is extremely doubtful that every al Qaeda agent would be caught, and an outbreak of anthrax or bubonic plague, the spread of deadly Sarin gas, the use of radiological weapons, or the detonation of a nuclear device could kill millions.

Richard A. Clarke, President Clinton's National Security Council adviser in charge of counterterrorism, said in an interview published in the *Washington Post* that Osama bin Laden's reach now extends to an astounding 45 countries. Yet he and his fanatical followers are not the only terrorists threatening the civilian populations of the world with WMD.

According to an article published on the BBC News Online website in February 1998, a safehouse belonging to a militant group called the German Red Army Faction was discovered in Paris in 1984. Inside the house, police found a laboratory used to manufacture the lethal botulism toxin. Israeli intelligence also suspect that the radical Palestinian terrorist group Hezbollah—and perhaps other militant anti-Israeli organizations—are now seeking to obtain chemical and biological weapons to use against Jewish civilians. Terrorist groups capable of using these insidious weapons are also known to be operating in Algeria,

Afghanistan, Chad, Colombia, Fiji, Japan, Jordan, Lebanon, Pakistan, Puerto Rico, Turkey, Uganda, and Venezuela.

Because the United States has thousands of miles of coastline where terrorists could land undetected, not to mention an all but open border with Canada, Americans are especially vulnerable to attacks employing WMD. Indeed, such attacks have already occurred. The bomb that exploded in the World Trade Center during the first terrorist attack on the complex in 1993 reportedly contained cyanide, but the chemical apparently evaporated in the explosion. The perpetrators of the attack turned out to be Islamic extremists, but many other domestic terrorist groups capable of the use of WMD are known to exist.

In 1984, members of the extremist Rajneesh sect based in Oregon used salmonella—a pathogenic bacteria—to infect salad bars in a number of local restaurants in an effort to influence elections in which cult members were running for office. Although no one was killed, 750 people were poisoned. Again, if the bacteria had been a more lethal, bioengineered strain, most of the people who became ill might instead have perished.

In 1995, four Minnesota members of an extremist group called the Patriots' Council were convicted of a plot to kill federal officials with a deadly toxin called ricin. In an article titled "The Rise of Terrorism" published on the website securitymanagement.com in August 2001, writer Stefan H. Leader reports that, "The plan was to mix the ricin with DMSO, a solvent that passes easily through the skin, and put the mixture on doorknobs and steering wheels where the victims would be sure to come in contact with it."

Today there are literally hundreds of hate groups, fanatical religious sects, cults, militias, ultra-radical environmentalists, and white supremacists in the United States who are willing to use any means—including WMD—to achieve their extremist goals. There are also thousands of unbalanced individuals—the post office worker with a grudge against his boss, the computer programmer who just got fired—ready and able to use violence to wreak revenge.

Although few of these fanatics possess the means to obtain or manufacture WMD, it would only take one madman with access to anthrax, bubonic plague, Sarin gas, radiological material, or any other toxin to instigate a massacre.

Suppose for a moment that Timothy McVeigh, the right-wing extremist who killed 168 people when he destroyed the Alfred P. Murrah Federal Building in Oklahoma City in 1995 with a 7,000-pound bomb, had had access to chemical or biological weapons. If, instead of a bomb, McVeigh had unleashed a newly bioengineered strain of anthrax, bubonic plague, smallpox, Sarin gas, or some other deadly toxin with no known cure in the building, the death toll might have been far higher—especially if the agent had spread through adjacent areas of Oklahoma City.

An even scarier candidate would have been the infamous Unabomber, Theodore Kaczynski. Kaczynski is a Harvard University graduate and former mathematics professor at the University of California at Berkeley. Using materials easily obtained from commercial sources, he manufactured his own bombs in a remote cabin in western Montana. His explosive devices became increasingly sophisticated during his reign of terror from 1978 to 1995. Although later diagnosed as a paranoid schizophrenic, Kaczynski was also a brilliant individual quite capable of formulating and employing WMD. In a letter to *The New York Times*, he allied himself with anarchists and radical environmentalists, and demanded the publication of his manifesto, entitled "Industrial Society and Its Future," a long-winded tirade against modern technology. Kaczynski's manifesto was published shortly afterward. But what would have been the consequences if the media had refused his demand to print his mad thesis? Would he have turned to more extreme measures—such as the use of WMD—to enforce his will? We know he had the brilliance, the access to toxic agent materials, and the seclusion necessary to formulate these deadly agents. The only thing we don't know is whether a chemical, biological, or radiological attack would have been his next demented step.

Kathleen C. Bailey, a former assistant director of the U.S. Arms Control and Disarmament Agency, is convinced that a terrorist could build a major biological arsenal with only $10,000 worth of equipment. Bailey points out that an extremist could cultivate trillions of deadly bacteria at little risk to him or herself, using gear no more sophisticated than a beer fermenter, a protein-based culture, a gas mask, and a plastic overgarment.

Although the use of WMD by terrorists is a very real and very frightening threat, scores of nations around the world are also working on chemical, biological, radiological, or nuclear weapons. And the number of countries is growing. In 1980, only one country, the Soviet Union, was believed to be developing such weapons. According to the U.S. Office of Technology Assessment, by 1989, 10 nations were suspected of working on WMD, and by 1995 the number had grown to 17, including Bulgaria, China, Cuba, Egypt, India, Iran, Iraq, Israel, Laos, Libya, North Korea, Russia, South Africa, South Korea, Syria, Taiwan, and Vietnam. A Pentagon report to Congress warned that political turmoil in the Middle East, the Balkans, and Southwest Asia might lead even more countries to develop—and perhaps use—WMD. Five of these countries—Iran, Iraq, Libya, North Korea, and Syria—have histories of hostility toward the United States, as well as sponsoring international terrorist acts.

Iraq poses a special threat. During the Persian Gulf War, Iraqi dictator Saddam Hussein ordered that Scud missiles with biological warheads be readied to be fired. These missiles were aimed at both Israel and the Saudi Arabian bases of the Coalition Forces allied against Iraq. Knowing that Saddam possessed deadly chemical and biological weapons, Coalition troops and Israeli civilians alike were issued gas masks and trained to use them. Only the threat of massive retaliation, including the use of nuclear weapons, prevented Saddam from loosing his deadly missiles.

> Scores of nations around the world are working on chemical, biological, radiological, or nuclear weapons.

Although the Iraqi madman did not deploy chemical or biological weapons during the Gulf War, he did use these toxins to kill tens of thousands of Iranian troops during the Iran-Iraq war, and to murder thousands of Kurds in northern Iraq when they rebelled against his regime. One of the conditions of Iraq's surrender following the country's defeat in the Gulf War was that UN weapons-inspection teams be allowed to enter Iraq and conduct a search for WMD, specifically stores of chemical and biological agents and the factories that produced them. The wily Saddam continuously blocked the efforts of inspection teams, and few supplies of toxins were uncovered and destroyed. The UN inspectors were eventually thrown out of the country before finding the vast quantities of biological weapons Iraq is believed to possess, including enough anthrax bacilli and botulism toxins to decimate the world's population.

Think about this for a moment. In a small outlaw country in the Middle East sits a madman with a history of torture, murder, and genocide, and the capability to wipe out the human race. What can we do to protect ourselves from WMD attacks from rogue nations, or fanatical foreign and domestic terrorists?

According to Leonard A. Cole, an adjunct professor of political science and an associate in the science, technology, and society program at Rutgers University, the answer is, very little. Cole believes that, "A large population cannot be protected against a biological attack. Vaccines can prevent some diseases, but unless the causative agent is known in advance, such a safeguard may be worthless. Antibiotics are effective against specific bacteria or classes of biological agents, but not against all."

Many scientists are also concerned about strains of bacteria that have become resistant to once-effective vaccines and antibiotics. This is happening naturally in many cases, but we should perhaps be even more worried that the scientists of some rogue nation somewhere in the world are developing deadly organisms that cannot be cured with any known medical treatments.

Are all potential attack organisms known? Absolutely not! Biotechnology has advanced to such a degree that rogue nations or terrorists could be developing chemical or biological agents tens or hundreds of times more deadly than those we now know of. We would simply have no defense against these new WMD.

What steps are being taken to protect innocent civilians from an attack employing WMD? Some, but not nearly enough. In the mid-1990s, then-Deputy Secretary of Defense John Deutch authored a report stating that biological agent detectors were "not being pursued adequately." Deutch went on to recommend a budget of $185 million for the development of biological and chemical weapons detection.

Cole also reveals that the Pentagon is sponsoring programs researching ion-trap mass spectrometry and laser-induced breakdown spectroscopy, technologies that search for chemical signatures of deadly agents in the air. Army scientists are simultaneously trying to find a "generic" detector that can identify classes of pathogens. The military has also established the Biological Integrated Detection System (BIDS), which can identify lethal agents by testing air samples. BIDS can now detect four deadly agents: anthrax, bubonic plague, botulism, and Staph bacteria. However, it remains uncertain whether BIDS can search out the full range of chemical and biological agents that terrorists or rogue nations might use against us.

Although the 1972 Biological Weapons Convention prohibited countries from researching, producing, or stockpiling chemical or biological WMD, terrorist groups and outlaw nations are undoubtedly ignoring the prohibition and producing bioweapons. How difficult would it be for terrorists or agents from rogue nations to smuggle WMD into the United States, Israel, the United Kingdom, France, Japan, or any other target country?

The answer, disturbingly, is not difficult at all. Chemical, biological, radiological, and nuclear weapons can be concealed in small containers. All the terrorists would need is a freighter—an oil tanker en route from the Persian Gulf to an American port, for instance—and then launch a small boat containing the WMD somewhere off our thousands of miles of coastline and land on some remote beach. Conspirators waiting on shore could then transport the weapon to any city in the United States. The same scenario applies to any country accessible by sea. WMD could also be smuggled in by air.

According to the Canadian Security Intelligence Service, "Although it is impossible to estimate the precise likelihood of a mass casualty terrorist attack using WMD, the technical obstacles to such an attack are by no means insuperable. It appears to be a case not of 'if' but rather of 'when' the next such event will occur."

The Canadian intelligence report goes on to state that, based on a combination of trends in both capabilities and motivations, "The threat appears to be growing. Despite increased attention to the threat since the Tokyo subway attack, society remains highly vulnerable to such attacks, the potential consequences of which are horrendous in the extreme."

Make no mistake. Terrorists will use chemical, biological, radiological, or nuclear weapons against the civilian population of the United States or some other country in the years to come. As the Canadian intelligence report points out, it is only a question of when and where, and how many millions will die.

ASTEROID IMPACTS
WITH EARTH

"The sky is falling, the sky is falling!" So cried Chicken Little in the old nursery fable, and even the children laughed. But the sky has fallen before, and it will again.

Skyfall loomed with the onrushing approach of the spaceborne object NEO 86 AZ. It appeared suddenly and without warning, like a comet. But it was no comet, no wandering iceball circling the sun in an elliptical orbit. It was an asteroid, a mote of rock adrift amid the planets.

A mote, that is, by cosmic standards. By the human frame of reference, it was a 2½-mile-long gray stone shaped like a piece of clay that's been squeezed in the middle before hardening. Its surface was pitted with small craters, the result of being pelted by other, smaller fragments of space debris.

Several billion years ago, the solar system numbered not nine but ten planets. The now-missing tenth planet occupied an orbital station between Mars and Jupiter, between the red planet and the titan planet. For some reason, the planet exploded. Possibly, its orbit was irregular, causing it to be torn to bits by the competing gravitational strains of Mars and Jupiter. Pieces of the disintegrated orb became the asteroid belt, a region of space rocks occupying the place where the planet had been, orbiting around the sun.

Every now and then, the intricate gravitational web of the sun, planets, and moons interacts in such a way as to nudge an asteroid from its orbit and send it wandering, sometimes plunging sunward, sometimes outward-bound to the stars.

And sometimes, earthward. Such visitors had impacted the planet before, most notably some 65 million years ago. That collision is memorialized by a crater 110 miles in diameter in Mexico's Yucatan peninsula, and in the absence of the dinosaurs, who suffered mass extinction in the aftermath of the meteor strike.

Until then, the dinosaurs had lasted hundreds of millions of years, successfully filling niches in land, sea, and sky. Humans have been around for less than one million years, of which only the last 5,000 years or so are known to history, and then imperfectly.

Somewhere in the asteroid belt, an intricate cosmic combination of gravitational factors came into play, nudging one space rock from its accustomed berth and sending it caroming off sunward. The object bulleted across the plane of planetary orbits, locked in a trajectory that would cause it to fall into the sun and be consumed. However, swinging around the sun on its eons-old orbit, Earth, by sheer chance, intersected the path of the oncoming asteroid.

Annihilation was first announced by Arizona's Lowell Observatory, whose astronomers had detected an anomalous object in a patch of star-studded space, which a telescopic-mounted camera was photographing. Meteor activity had been seen in the quadrant, streaks visible to the naked eye in that patch of night sky, prompting the astronomers to inquire more closely into the area.

The same gravitational minuet in the asteroid belt had loosed more than a few fragments of space rock earthward. The forerunners were small things, baseball- and basketball-size, flashing into incandescence as they burst into flame in Earth's atmosphere and were consumed. Photographic plates of the area detected a blurred streak that persisted for several nights running. Study revealed an object hurtling into the immediate vicinity of planet Earth. The object was named NEO 86 AZ, for Near Earth Object 86 Arizona, in honor of the state whose observatory first detected it.

The calculus of trajectories being an exact science, a number of researchers analyzing the data of the intruder's path reached the same conclusion, that the asteroid was on a collision course with Earth. None of the researchers was eager to claim the fame of having reached this conclusion first, since it lent itself to the worst kind of sensational headlines and media exploitation. But the numbers were hard, the conclusion inescapable: NEO 86 was going to impact Earth. The collision was imminent, a matter of a few weeks. Time enough to stir up panic, but nowhere near enough time to begin to cope with the threat. What could be done?

Blow it up with nuclear missiles? The United States's atomic missiles were designed to hit targets on the planet, not in space. Before weapons could be fitted and programmed to home in on the asteroid, it would already have struck. Many government high-ups were unconvinced that the asteroid would even hit the planet, pointing out that the odds against it were, well, astronomical. Others argued that such impacts had happened before. Politicians responded to the sizeable proportion of the population that feared the danger of atomic missiles launched spaceward more than they did some hypothetical asteroid strike. Even without the obstructionists, time was too short to do anything but sit tight and hold on while NEO 86 AZ made its final approach.

Chicken Little didn't seem so silly any more.

Occupying a front-row seat for the show were the occupants of the International Space Station, a crew of a dozen or so astronauts and cosmonauts posted to the space-based platform circling in geosynchronous orbit above the planet. They witnessed NEO 86 AZ fall out of infinity, plummeting toward the blue planet. Though the world is four fifths water, it managed to hit land: the south central region of the United States. Impacting with the explosive energy of a thermonuclear device, the object punched a hole in the lower half of middle America. Shock waves from the strike thrust new mountains into being in the north central states, up into Canada. Cracks in the landmass opened all the way to the Gulf of Mexico, causing flooding of Biblical proportion that created a central sea reaching all the way to Kansas.

Here was disaster on a planetary scale. Atmospheric disturbances cut off all contact between the space station and earthbound Mission Control—if it still existed. The pall of dust and smoke from the crash obscured the western hemisphere, blotting it out to the space station's occupants, blindly wheeling around the hulk of a ruined world.

———————————■———————————

Asteroids vary in size, from small stones to giant chunks of rock many miles across. Normally, the objects remain within the two known asteroid belts—one between the sun and Mercury and the other between Earth and Mars—where they pose no danger to Earth. Sometimes, though, as a result of orbital anomalies, such as the gravitational pull of another planet, an asteroid will veer out of its regular orbit. Over the millennia, the sudden change in the course of asteroids has put many on a direct trajectory toward Earth.

Although recent movies and novels have awakened the public to the possibility that a Near Earth Object (NEO) could strike the planet tomorrow, or next year, or during the lifetime of your children, few people take the threat seriously. Most believe that it's only the stuff of fantasy, an implausible scenario from the minds of science-fiction writers.

Wrong! The threat that a NEO could impact the earth, causing such a massive upheaval of our ecosystems, atmosphere, and climate that almost all life forms on the planet would be wiped out—including the human species—is not just a possibility, it is a very real probability. The only question is when such a titanic extinction event will occur again.

In this age of satellites, moon landings, the incredible Hubble Space Telescope, and deep space probes by robot spacecraft, most of us assume that an asteroid could not be on a collision course with our planet without astronomers detecting the object. This is a fallacy. In reality, only a small fraction of space surrounding the earth is now being monitored for NEOs. Astronomers estimate that currently as many as 2,000 asteroids larger than one-half mile in diameter—many far bigger and more lethal—are in the earth-crossing orbit. Yet only about half of these have so far been detected and tracked. None of these NEOs appears to be on a direct trajectory for our planet, but what about the estimated 90 percent of asteroids that have not yet been spotted? An NEO that could strike the earth in the next 24 hours may well be out there. Scientists readily admit that they simply cannot predict such an event.

THEY'RE OUT THERE

Are asteroid and meteor collisions with our blue planet rare? Hardly. In recent years, almost 150 large impact craters have been discovered through satellite probes and technological advances in ground-based geology, and several more craters are discovered each year. These impact craters are only the tip of the iceberg. From the study of other bodies in the solar system, we know that in past geologic eras, the earth was bombarded by at least 100 times the number of asteroids and meteors that now strike our planet. The planet Mars and our own moon are prime examples: Their surfaces are pitted with the craters caused by asteroid impacts. Although the surfaces of these bodies have remained largely unchanged over billions of years, the surface of the earth has undergone radical transformations due to the movement of crustal plates, volcanic eruptions, ice ages, changes in sea level, and the crater-concealing buildup of soil, sand, and other sediments. The dilemma facing geologists today is how to detect asteroid impact sites long buried by the natural geological processes of our vibrant planet. Some of the larger craters are so huge that they can only be detected by satellite imaging.

According to David Morrison, planetary astronomer and Director of Space at the NASA Ames Research Center, "The most probable warning for a kilometer-scale impact is zero. The first we would likely know of such a strike is when we feel the ground shake and watch the fireball rising above the horizon."

Morrison points out that our government has not funded large-scale searches, but surveys of the sky are still being carried out by astronomers searching for NEOs on a collision course with our planet. The LINEAR search program of the MIT Lincoln Lab, in cooperation with NASA and the U.S. Air Force, employs two telescopes in New Mexico searching for incoming asteroids and meteorites. The LINEAR search has discovered more NEOs in the past three years than all other previous searches combined. Other groups searching space for approaching objects include the Near-Earth Asteroid Tracking (NEAT) program in Hawaii, operated jointly by the Jet Propulsion Laboratory in California and the U.S. Air Force, and the Spacewatch Project conducted by astronomers at the University of Arizona.

The Spacewatch project employs both 0.9 meter and 1.8 meter telescopes to study the Centaur, Trojan, Main-Belt, Trans-Neptunian, and Earth-approaching asteroid populations. Recent probes have discovered several asteroids that may pose a threat to the earth, including asteroid 1997 XF[11], which will pass close to the earth in the year 2028; asteroid 1998 KY[26], which passed close enough for radar observations to be taken, and which has the fastest rotation of any known body in the solar system; and asteroid 2000 BF[19], which has the potential to collide with the earth in 2022. Other searches for NEOs are being conducted by the Lowell Observatory Near-Earth Object Search (LONEOS) in Flagstaff, Arizona, by the Catalina Sky Survey in Tucson, and by various foreign governments and amateur astronomers.

Even with all these powerful telescopes searching space for NEOs, astronomers believe that they have discovered no more than half of the asteroids greater than a mile in diameter, and hundreds of smaller objects also remain undetected. One of these objects was an asteroid named 1989 FC⁹, which passed within 435,000 miles of the earth 12 years ago. Relative to the dimensions of space, this is razor-close. Although the object was less than half a mile in diameter, if it had impacted a land surface, it would have produced a crater almost 22 miles in diameter and caused a geological and atmospheric upheaval unimaginable to modern humanity.

If 1989 FC⁹ had landed in the sea, a tsunami over 1,000 feet high would have swept inland over the surrounding shore areas. If it had impacted the North Sea between England and Norway, for example, the port cities in both countries, including London and Oslo, would have been inundated by an immense tsunami and destroyed, drowning millions of people. The coasts of Sweden, Finland, Russia, Latvia, Estonia, and Lithuania—all life and structures—would have been wiped away. The coastal area in the north of France would also have disappeared beneath the skyscraping wall of water, which would have surged far inland across Denmark, Germany, Belgium, and the Netherlands.

New research indicates that NEOs with the destructive power of nuclear weapons strike the earth every couple of centuries. Yet because six out of seven explode above the world's oceans, few were noticed by humans before the advent of modern NEO detection technology. The space age brought a new recognition of the frequency and threat of NEO impacts. In 1972, a bus-size rock skimmed so low through the earth's atmosphere that tourists in Wyoming's Grand Tetons Mountains were able to photograph the object. Fortunately, the NEO ricocheted back into space, like a stone skipping over water. Had the asteroid struck directly, it would have caused a hydrogen-bomb–size explosion over Canada. Several years later, during the 1990s, an Air Force satellite

> Most scientists conclude that there is a significant threat of future impact—when and at what scale, no one knows.

detected the explosion of a NEO over the Pacific. Every year, hundreds of asteroids the size of a loaf of bread burn through the atmosphere and strike different locations around the world. Although most fall into the sea, some strike populated areas.

Most scientists studying NEOs conclude that there is a significant threat of future impact—when and at what scale, no one knows—and that governments should begin planning strategies to destroy or deflect incoming asteroids or meteoroids. Based on the latest research, astronomers believe that there may be up to 8,000 objects over a quarter of a mile in diameter—and perhaps an astounding 1.5 million from 150 to 200 feet across—in an earth-crossing orbit.

The question naturally arises: "How much damage could a rock only 200 feet in diameter do to a planet as large as the earth?" The answer is that an asteroid 35 feet in diameter striking the earth at a typical entry velocity of 12 miles per second would produce an explosion comparable to the detonation of a nuclear weapon. Thus, the impact of an asteroid no bigger than a house could obliterate any large city on earth, along with all life for miles around. The impact of a larger object—a half-mile or more in diameter—could destroy all life within entire states or foreign countries, killing tens of millions if the impact occurred in a densely populated area.

According to David Morrison, the greatest threat to human life would come from the impact of an asteroid roughly two kilometers in diameter. An object of this size colliding with our planet would result in the release of approximately one million megatons of energy, equivalent to the simultaneous detonation of tens of thousands of nuclear weapons. The explosion, shock waves, fireballs, earthquakes, tsunamis, and cold, dark "impact winter" that followed would threaten most higher life forms on the planet, including humans.

On average, an asteroid of this size collides with the earth once every 500,000 to 1 million years. The next impact could come tomorrow, or many millennia from now. All we can be certain of is that a huge NEO will strike the earth sometime in the future—just as they have repeatedly in the past—causing massive destruction in the blink of an eye.

CAN WE PREVENT A STRIKE?

How much warning will we have? With half of even the largest NEOs still undiscovered—and 90 percent of smaller objects still hidden in the vastness of space—the answer is that we would likely have no warning at all. One of the strongest proponents of initiating a program of asteroid detection and defense was the world-renowned physicist Edward Teller—father of the H-bomb—who argued that we should initiate experiments, including nuclear tests, designed to learn more about how to deflect or destroy asteroids and comets before they impact the earth. Other scientists insist that the chance of impact of an asteroid large enough to bring about the end of life on earth is remote at worst. They point out that past great extinctions thought to be caused by NEO impacts occurred tens or hundreds of millions of years apart.

Or did they? Just after dawn on the morning of June 30, 1908, a fireball raced through the earth's atmosphere and exploded above the remote area of the Tunguska River in Siberia. The titanic energy of the explosion—equivalent to the force of a 15-megaton nuclear bomb—flattened hundreds of square miles of forest, and set the shattered trees ablaze. Although the extraterrestrial object—a stony asteroid, judging by the evidence—exploded an estimated four miles above the ground, the detonation was so immense that it was recorded on seismographs around the world. The sound of the ear-splitting blast was heard 300 miles from the impact scene, and eyewitnesses more than 100 miles away reported seeing a brilliant fireball in the sky. People almost 40 miles from the site of the blast were thrown to the ground—many knocked unconscious—while nearer the scene, vast herds of wild reindeer were blown to smithereens.

Imagine if the impact had occurred over New York City—as it easily could have. It would have killed every human being in the metropolitan area, and devastated large sections of Connecticut, New Jersey, and Pennsylvania. Only luck put the explosion in a remote and unpopulated corner of the globe.

Sixty-five million years ago, the dinosaurs—which had survived on Earth over hundreds of millions of years—suddenly died out, as did

76 percent of all other fauna and flora on the planet. The dinosaurs and other animal and plant species did not die of disease, predation, or failure to evolve. They were annihilated by an asteroid.

There is overwhelming geological and paleological evidence that past asteroid or meteor impacts upon the earth have wiped out up to 97 percent of all life forms on our planet. Scientists generally agree that no fewer than five major extinctions of life on earth have occurred during the past 500 million years. The first occurred during the Ordovician period approximately 440 million years ago, when more than 85 percent of the species on earth suddenly became extinct. The second mass ex-tinction took place at the end of the Devonian period around 370 million years ago, when an estimated 82 percent of all fauna and flora ceased to exist. The third and most massive extinction we know of occurred 245 million years ago at the end of the Permian period, when a staggering 96 percent of all life forms on earth suddenly died off. Thirty-seven million years later, near the end of the Triassic period, the fourth planet-wide extinction took place, wiping out 76 percent of all species that existed at that time.. The fifth mass extinction is perhaps the most well known because it killed off the dinosaurs. The event is called the "K-T extinction," because it marks the boundary between the Creta-ceous period (K) and the Tertiary period (T).

Can we be certain that asteroid impacts with the earth caused these five massive extinctions? No. There are other explanations, including titanic volcanic eruptions and sudden changes in the earth's climate caused by such natural events as ice ages. Still, research pioneered by a group of scientists led by Luis and Walter Alvarez at the University of California at Berkeley provides compelling evidence that the massive extinction event that wiped out the dinosaurs 65 million years ago was almost certainly caused by an asteroid impact with the earth.

In the 1970s, Walter Alvarez was studying rock formations in Gubbio, Italy, when he came across an unusual layer of clay marking the boundary point between the Cretaceous and Tertiary periods. What made the clay layer remarkable was that it contained an abnormal spike in the amount of the rare element iridium. The same high density of iridium was later discovered in K-T boundary stratum—layers of rock formed over the ages—in Denmark, New Zealand, and other areas of the world, indicating that the shower of iridium had been global in scale.

The spike revealed that the clay contained roughly 30 times the normal level of iridium found in other layers of stratum. Iridium is an extremely rare element on the earth's surface because it bonds with iron and long ago was segregated into the planet's liquid iron core.

Iridium may occasionally rise from the earth's core during volcanic eruptions, but this is a rather infrequent occurrence, and it is doubtful that even the most titanic eruption could have spewed out enough iridium to account for the heavy concentration of the element found in the K-T boundary stratum around the world.

The main source of iridium in the present age is outer space. Cosmic dust, asteroids, and other extraterrestrial objects carry the element to the surface of the earth. However, this rain of iridium is slow and almost always, evenly paced levels never approach the high density discovered by the Alvarez team. In addition to the iridium, large amounts of soot were found within the clay layer, leading the researchers to speculate that immense global fires had burned across the entire planet following an asteroid impact.

A third clue was the presence in the clay layer of what geologists call "shocked quartz." Ordinary quartz can be physically altered in this way only by being suddenly exposed to extreme temperatures and pressure— exactly the conditions that would be caused by the impact of an immense asteroid with the earth. Later research revealed high iridium levels, soot, and shocked quartz in K-T boundary layers in Denmark, New Zealand, and other areas on every continent, indicating that the shower of iridium had been global.

Luis Alvarez felt there was only one answer: 65 million years ago, at the end of the Cretaceous period, a huge asteroid had collided with the earth, releasing immense amounts of iridium, starting global forest fires and sending trillions of tons of dust, gases, and debris into the atmosphere to block out the light and heat of the sun. Since the dating of the clay layer corresponded exactly with the extinction of the dinosaurs, Alvarez theorized that the immense reptiles had not been killed off by disease or by the natural processes of the earth—such as an ice age—

but by the sudden impact of an asteroid that altered our climate, obliterating most plant and animal species.

Alvarez's theory was at first viewed with skepticism. "Show us the crater," many scientists argued. If an asteroid large enough to radically alter our climate overnight had struck the earth, the crater it left behind should be huge. Yet, no such crater dating from that time had ever been discovered.

Then, in 1990, a scientist named Alan Hildebrand happened to be going over some old data collected by a group of geophysicists searching for oil in the Yucatan area of Mexico. As he studied the data, Hildebrand noticed a deeply buried ring-shaped structure roughly 110 miles in diameter. The geologist recognized that the circular formation might well be the site of an asteroid impact, and he made his findings known to the scientific community. The crater, named Chicxulub after a local village, was later dated as being 65 million years old—exactly the same time frame as the K-T extinction event—and its size corresponded with the impact scar that would have been created if a six-mile-wide asteroid had struck the earth. An asteroid of that size would have created worldwide devastation severe enough to wipe out the dinosaurs and 76 percent of the other animal and plant species then living on Earth. Luis Alvarez now had solid evidence to support his theory that an asteroid impact with the earth had led to the dinosaurs' extinction, and opened the door for the evolution of the human species from a small, nocturnal, rodentlike mammal to the dominant species on the planet.

Research indicates that the asteroid that killed the dinosaurs struck the planet's surface at approximately 62,000 miles per hour. The impact caused a blast equivalent to the detonation of millions of tons of TNT. The effect of the impact was devastating. The asteroid itself and much of the surrounding rock in the impact area was totally vaporized. Fireballs and molten material thrown into the atmosphere rained down upon the earth, incinerating trees and other vegetation for thousands of miles. Enormous tidal waves over a thousand feet high swept across the Caribbean Sea, flooding scores of low-lying islands and surging across the shores of North and South America as far inland as what is today central Alabama. The incredible force of the asteroid smashing into the crust of the earth caused a chain of unimaginably strong earth-quakes that tore apart large areas, reshaping the landscape of the planet.

Millions of plants and animals were killed or destroyed instantly. But the worst was yet to come. The immense amount of dust, debris, soot, steam, and gases ejected into the atmosphere by the titanic impact darkened the sky, blocking the sun and casting the earth into a long, cold "impact winter."

Photosynthesis, the process by which plants derive energy, was violently disrupted, and the plant-eating dinosaurs suddenly had no food. As the plant-eaters died out, so did the predator species that fed upon them, such as the well-known Tyrannosaurus Rex. Only the smaller scavengers like birds and mammals, able to find food from a variety of sources, survived.

The effect on sea life was equally disastrous. Massive underwater currents created by the impact brought a decrease in oxygen levels in the water, and low-oxygen seawater rose to the surface. Torrential acid rains caused by the impact brought on a sudden increase in the acidity of the seawater. This combination led to the rapid death of plankton—the tiny organisms that are the foundation of the marine food chain—and most of the marine reptiles, shelled sea animals, and early species of fish died out.

The same scenario may well await humanity. NEOs impact the earth far more frequently than most of us imagine. Pea-size meteorites, large enough to shatter your body if you are unlucky enough to be in their path, strike the earth every six minutes. Once every hour, walnut-size meteorites strike our planet. Grapefruit-size meteorites that could turn your house into a pile of smoldering rubble burn through our atmosphere an average of once every 10 hours, while a basketball-size object with enough explosive power to destroy a skyscraper strikes the surface of the earth perhaps once a month. An asteroid 150 to 200 feet in diameter—large enough to destroy the state of New Jersey—impacts our planet on an average of once every 100 years. Monster NEOs capable of wiping out all life on Earth burn through our atmosphere at intervals ranging from 500,000 to tens of millions of years.

Since the last known huge asteroid impact occurred 65 million years ago, it is an inescapable fact that another massive impact looms over the earth like the guillotine blade over the neck of Marie Antoinette. Whether the titanic life-ending event will come tomorrow, or during the lifetime of your children, or 50 million years from now, it is impossible to know.

If a NEO the size of the Chicxulub asteroid were to strike a populated area of the earth tomorrow, hundreds of millions of people would be instantly killed. Tens of millions more would perish shortly afterwards in the resulting fires, earthquakes, and tsunamis.

Those who survived the immediate aftermath of the asteroid strike would soon either starve or freeze to death. As the dust, debris, and gasses from the impact saturated the atmosphere and blocked out sunlight, an impact winter would set in. Food sources such as wheat, corn, rice, and other grains would not be able to survive the absence of photosynthesis, and crops all over the planet would wither in the fields. Deprived of pasturelands and feed, meat-producing animals such as cattle, pigs and chickens would soon perish.

There is no doubt that somewhere out there in deep, dark space, an asteroid is on an impact trajectory with the earth. The only question is when it will strike, and if the human species will survive.

MASSIVE VOLCANIC
ERUPTIONS

World's Greatest Fireworks Display!

That's how the news media labeled the eruption of Mount Yaanek, a volcanic cone on a remote island off the Alaskan coast. The setting was picturesque, the pyrotechnics were spectacular, and except for a displaced fishing village and some trappers and traders, no one had been seriously affected. Admittedly, the several thousand residents of Bellew Point, on the coast some 40 miles south of Yaanek Isle, were understandably apprehensive about living so close to a live volcano. However, the increased business done by the town to provide food, shelter, and recreation for the press and TV crews dispatched to cover the story helped take some of the sting out of living in the shadow of Mount Yaanek.

The island was dominated by the cone of what had once been assumed to be an extinct volcano. On the leeward, inshore side, a small fishing village of several large families, numbering about 100 people, had taken root. The last decade or two had proven that Yaanek was not extinct. This area of Alaska was known to be seismically unstable, with several small and insignificant temblors per year. Once every half-century or so, a more severe quake struck, demolishing a few coastal villages.

In recent years, the Yaanek region began exhibiting signs of extensive though as yet minor seismic activity. At the epicenter was the volcanic cone itself. Records showed that, while Yaanek had been relatively quiet during the last hundred years, it had experienced significant activity before. Apparently, such activity was about to resume. Increasing periods of cyclic seismic activity centered on Yaanek was accompanied by indications of imminent eruption, such as the appearance of geysers and hot springs at the foot of the mountain, and a buildup of acidic sulfur in the streams and rivulets running out to sea.

The earth shrugged, knocking the inhabitants of Yaanek's fishing village out of their beds and on the run. As they hastily abandoned their ramshackle homes, sailing for the safety of the mainland shore, a line of smoke rose from somewhere in the interior of the volcanic cone. Vulcanologists, scientists who study volcanoes, now had a newcomer to contemplate. From around the world, teams of scientists arrived to monitor Mount Yaanek on its path toward eruption. They operated out of Bellew Point, establishing forward bases on the island and the nearby mainland coast.

CHAPTER 3: MASSIVE VOLCANIC ERUPTIONS

Preceded by a series of tremors, a line of fire suddenly leaped up from the lip of the volcano. From the mouth of the cone poured smoke, ash, and debris, climbing and spreading across the sky. The great looming black cloud was underlit by the fiery flames and flashes. Red-hot magma spewed from the cone, dribbling down its sides like hot wax, winding in serpentine ribbons of living fire down the mountain, across the island, and into the sea, where clouds of superheated steam poured up as lava plunged into icy waters.

The imagery was spectacular, luring a large cadre of news media to cover the story. The public was hungry for stories that didn't deal with war and terror, so the pageantry of fiery Mount Yaanek amid Alaskan seas was prominently featured in nightly news broadcasts and front-page tabloid photos.

After about two and a half weeks, the eruptions trailed off, the magma flow dribbled off to a trickle, and the smoke clouds thinned. The pictures weren't so spectacular anymore, prompting the news teams to begin making arrangements for their return home.

Then Mount Yaanek blew its top.

To those in Bellew Point, the sudden explosion sounded like the crack of doom. The town, the landscape, shook like a gong struck by a mallet. The blast was felt as much as heard. Actually, it was a series of blasts, each coming so closely after the other that they sounded like a continuous bellowing roar. Like a genie freed from a bottle, masses of smoke and ash billowed out from the crater mouth, belching out an inverted mountain of roiling blackness that swiftly filled the sky from horizon to horizon.

The town of Bellew Point had been built on the flat top of a promontory overlooking the sea, so it was safe from the tsunami generated by the volcanic tremors. Every boat in the harbor was smashed to splinters by the giant waves that hammered them against the rocky shore, as were the docks, wharves, and warehouses lining the waterfront.

Mount Yaanek was a howitzer, firing off red-hot, house-size boulders for dozens of miles around, peppering land and sea with fiery bombs whose smoky trails arrowed out from the volcano like the limbs of a multi-tentacled fire monster. The blasts were so great that they split the volcano's eastern, shoreward face down the middle, and the plunging crevasse blazed with white-hot incandescence as lava spilled from it, splashing down the mountainside toward the boiling sea. Fat flakes of gray ash rained down from towering black clouds, spilling a blizzard down on Bellew Point, burying it and its inhabitants—and the press cadre, most of whom had been asphyxiated in the choking clouds or crushed under the aerial bombardment of molten rocks.

Later, scientists would learn what had happened. Mount Yaanek, in previous centuries an active volcano, had subsided, its fires dimming. A plug of molten lava had cooled, corking the volcano. Recently, shifting internal pressures in the crust below the island had opened fresh paths for subcrustal molten magma to climb, filling the volcanic tube until balked by the hardened rock plug. Increasing pressure had forced thin streams of magma through flaws in the rock, leading to the initial series of eruptions, spectacular but unthreatening, which had caught the world's fancy.

A massive chunk of solid rock, thrust upward by the lava flowing into the volcano tube, had become lodged in its mouth, below the bottom of the rocky plug, blocking the pressurized gases and magma that the cracks in the plug had vented. With its escape route blocked, the safety valve had, in effect, been closed.

Pressure built up until the rocky plug crumbled, propelled upward as the volcano blew its top. Now, the stumpy remains of Mount Yaanek continued to spew masses of smoke, ash, and magma, showing no signs of stopping. So great was the eruption that it was theorized that somewhere underground a major fault had opened in the earth's crust, enabling the release of unprecedented volumes of molten magma.

Ominously, while Yaanek continued to rage unabated, some 300 miles to the south, in a coastal mountain range, another inactive volcano, Mount Nehleh, began to smoke and shake. Nehleh lay along the same tectonic plate edge as Yaanek, indicating that massive strains and pressures might be causing new fault lines to develop in the earth's crust, leading to the creation of a potentially earthshaking line of new volcanoes, a volcanic belt stretching from Alaska down through Canada into the numerous dormant volcanoes of the Cascade mountains bordering the Pacific Coast. These were populous regions, and their citizens were no longer so pleased by the diversion offered by a "fireworks display" in the backyards of Seattle, Portland, Vancouver ....

CHAPTER 3: MASSIVE VOLCANIC ERUPTIONS

As cataclysmic as the eruption of Mount Yaanek had been, something far worse appeared to be in the offing.

———————————————■———————————————

To most of us, volcanic eruptions such as the May 1980 explosion of Mount St. Helens in Washington State are of little more than passing interest. They invoke a certain amount of excitement—perhaps even a degree of foreboding—but most of these events soon fade from our consciousness. Our sanguine view of volcanoes flows from the fact that—while there have been large eruptions in relatively recent history— there have not been any truly massive eruptions for several millennia.

Does this mean that these life-threatening events will not occur in future? No, and it is both foolish and dangerous to believe that volcanoes do not present a very real threat not only to humanity but to every species of animals and plants on Earth. Indeed, the greatest extinction of life in the history of our planet was caused by violent volcanic eruptions that continued unabated for an astounding million years. It happened 250 million years ago, when volcanoes rising above a fiery fissure in the earth's crust began erupting lava, gases, volcanic bombs, pumice, and ash across the plains of Siberia.

Isotopic dating of rock samples indicate that the eruptions coincided with the mass extinction of 95 percent of all species on earth at the end of the Permian period. Paleontologists call the event "The Great Dying," for fossil records show that not only individual species but entire families of animals, plants, insects, and marine life suddenly ceased to exist.

In recent years, researchers have advanced many theories to explain the Permian extinction. These have included meteor impacts, greenhouse warming, ice-age cooling, sea-level changes, and ocean stagnation. However, according to Paul Renne, director of the Berkeley Geochronology Center at the University of California, such indiscriminate carnage could not have been caused by any imaginable calamity other than the titanic Siberian eruptions. "None of these agents of doom comes as close to explaining what happened at the end of the Permian as the rampant, prolonged volcanism that created the terrace-like formations known as the Siberian Traps (from *trappa*, the Swedish word for stairs)."

Respected scientist and writer J. Madeleine Nash writes, "These traps are composed mainly of glassy basalt laid down by huge rivers of flowing lava. But amid the basalt, which extends over an area of a million square miles, scientists have also found telltale pieces of tuff, a type of rock indicative of powerful explosions."

Many scientists, including Renne and Nash, now accept the theory that the extended volcanism may well have spewed so much sulfur dioxide and other gases into the atmosphere that the pollutants blocked out a large percentage of the sunlight that normally reaches the earth and led to dramatic cooling of the climate. This, in turn, would have brought on an immense increase in the amount of seawater trapped in polar ice and a consequent drop in global sea levels.

Hundreds of thousands of years of nonstop volcanism would also have produced a continuous deluge of acid rain that would have decimated both plant and animal life all over the world.

THE POWER BENEATH

While scientists continue to debate what triggered The Great Dying at the end of the Permian era, the most widely accepted theory is that the root cause was the massive volcanic eruptions in Siberia. Volcanism of equal or greater magnitude could occur again at any time, for deep in the core of the planet is a fiery cauldron that is continuously sending plumes of molten magma upward toward the surface of the earth. To fully comprehend the threat to human life posed by volcanoes, one must first understand the unimaginably powerful forces that create volcanoes.

The earth has a radius of 3,959 miles and is made up of four main layers: the solid inner core, composed mostly of iron with an estimated temperature of some 6,000 degrees Celsius; the liquid outer core, made up almost entirely of iron and only a little cooler; and the relatively plastic mantle, composed of iron, magnesium, aluminum, silicon, oxygen, and silicate compounds, which makes up most of the earth's mass and maintains a temperature believed to be well over 1,000 degrees Celsius.

Finally, at the surface of the earth, is the solid crust on which life exists. The crust ranges from 3 to 60 miles in thickness, has a mean surface temperature of 0 degrees Celsius, and is made up of less-dense calcium, sodium, and aluminum-silicate minerals. Being relatively cold, the crust is brittle, and thus may be fractured by earthquakes or punctured by volcanoes. The crust is broken up into eight major tectonic plates—both continental and oceanic—as well as several minor slabs. To envision what these plates look like, think of the irregularly cracked shell of an egg. The plates have random sizes and shapes. For instance, the Cocos plate off the western coast of Central America is only 1,400 miles wide, while the Pacific plate is almost 9,000 miles in width. These plates move constantly across the surface of the earth, thought by many scientists to be driven by heat-generated convection currents deep within the planet. The plates slide along the outer fringe of the plastic mantle like dishes slipping across a slanted, greasy tabletop.

Vastly different geological processes take place where two or more plates meet. Plates may slip along beside each other, often storing up energy for decades or centuries, and then suddenly lurch forward, producing earthquakes. Such an event caused the infamous San Francisco earthquake of 1906.

Other plates may press against each other, forcing the land mass behind to rise in mountain chains, just as wrinkles form when you push two pieces of cloth together. The highest mountain range in the world, the Himalayas, was created when the Indian-Australian plate slowly moved into the southern edge of the Eurasian plate tens of millions of years ago.

The third type of plate boundary interaction is called subduction. In this case, one plate slides under another, descending ever deeper into the increasing hot mantle until the crust becomes molten. Most of the crust will continue downward to be recycled. However, some of the molten material will rise upward through fissures to the earth's surface, creating volcanoes.

There are three distinct types of volcanoes: shield volcanoes, cinder cones, and composite volcanoes. Shield volcanoes are formed when a large amount of free-flowing magma (lava) is ejected from a central vent, or sometimes several vents, and spreads out widely across the slopes below.

One of the most famous volcanoes in the world—Mauna Loa in Hawaii—is an example of a shield volcano. Cinder cones are created when successive eruptions deposit tephra—a collection of ash, pumice, rock fragments, and volcanic bombs—around the central vent.

Composite volcanoes are the most dangerous, exploding in violent eruptions and ejecting lava, tephra, and gases from a vent at or near the peak. These volcanic materials feed up from a reservoir of molten magma within or below the mountain. Typically, composite volcanoes are towering, cone-shaped mountains that dominate the surrounding lowlands.

The majority of composite volcanoes form above subduction zones. For instance, the infamous "Ring of Fire"—a rough circle of active volcanoes surrounding the Pacific Ocean—exists because most of the land masses bordering the Pacific have subduction zones off their coasts. These areas include Japan, the Southwest Pacific island chains, the west coasts of South and Central America, far-eastern Russia, Alaska, and the Pacific Northwest of the United States and Canada.

Huge, prolonged volcanic eruptions may have caused the Great Dying and perhaps other massive extinctions. However, it is sobering to think that volcanic eruptions far smaller in size and duration could pose a very real threat to life on Earth. An example is the eruption of the volcanic island of Thera (Santorini) in the Aegean Sea in approximately 1650 B.C.E., one of the largest volcanic eruptions in the past 10,000 years.

Scientists estimate that the volcano spewed out about seven cubic miles of magma, and ejected a column of volcanic debris and gases well into the stratosphere. Ash from the eruption fell over thousands of square miles of the eastern Mediterranean and Turkey, undoubtedly destroying countless crop fields and causing widespread starvation. Archeologists also believe that the eruption probably brought about the end of the Minoan civilization centered on the nearby island of Crete. The Minoans were perhaps the most highly advanced culture on Earth from around 3000 B.C.E. until the devastating eruption of

Thera. They were intellectually advanced, dominated Mediterranean commerce, and exerted sociological and economic influence over the surrounding islands and continents. Then Thera blew apart, and the Minoan civilization disintegrated. Thereafter, the most advanced facets of civilization—learning and knowledge, architecture, mastery of the sea, and sophisticated forms of sociology and government—shifted to Greece.

The eruption of Thera and the subsequent destruction of the Minoan civilization are thought by many scientists and historians to have given birth to the legend of the vanished island civilization of Atlantis, first recorded by Plato. This titanic volcanic event may also have directly contributed to the Exodus of the Jews from Egypt by bringing about the calamitous natural disasters that devastated Egypt at exactly the same time, and which forced the pharaoh to release the tens of thousands of Jews he held in virtual slavery.

ASH AND CHAOS

To put the destruction of the advanced Minoan civilization into modern perspective, picture a volcanic eruption in the northern hemisphere huge enough to wipe out the major cites of the United States, Europe, and Asia; laying waste to crops and killing off tens of millions of meat-producing animals; destroying regional commerce and transportation systems by making it impossible to ship goods or travel via ash-covered roads, railways, and airports; and causing a hemisphere-wide communications blackout as fiery debris knocked out land lines and clouds of ash so saturate the atmosphere that wireless transmissions are severely disrupted. The result would be the total collapse of most, if not all, societies in the northern hemisphere. We would be returned to—at best—Medieval times.

With the breakdown in supply, distribution, and transportation of foodstuffs, supermarkets would be abandoned, and people would be forced to resort to the barter system to obtain ever-shrinking food and fuel supplies. Wars would erupt between the rich and the poor, looting would become rampant, and law and order would break down into uncontrollable social chaos.

Only the strong would survive: perhaps well-armed rogue military units or the super-rich, able to pay private armies. The center of civilization would most likely shift to the southern hemisphere—to Buenos Aires, Rio de Janeiro, Capetown, or Sydney. Although the volcanic clouds would eventually move south of the equator, the effect on South America, southern Africa, Australia, New Zealand, and the island chains of the southern hemisphere would be far less severe than the devastation in North America, Europe, and mainland Asia.

Conversely, if a titanic volcanic eruption were to occur in the southern hemisphere—most likely on one of the volcanically active Indonesian islands or along the Ring of Fire running up the west coast of South America—the devastation would force tens if not hundreds of millions of starving, desperate refugees to flee to the northern hemisphere. How could we feed them? How could we house them? How could the United States, Europe, or Asia prevent such stupendous numbers of refugees from causing ungovernable turmoil on a scale we cannot even begin to imagine?

> Volcanoes often give off early signs that they are becoming active, but others erupt with little or no warning.

While it is possible that looming titanic volcanic eruptions could wipe out humankind —along with all other life forms on Earth— smaller volcanic events also pose a grave threat to densely populated areas of the earth, with economic and sociological consequences that could impact civilizations in every corner of the world. Dozens of large cities and crowded suburban areas are situated in volcanic danger zones along the Ring of Fire, as well as other volcanically active regions around the world. Volcanoes often give off early signs that they are becoming active, but others erupt with little or no warning. If one of the many volcanoes located near heavily populated areas were to explode suddenly, the eruptions would reduce nearby skyscrapers, cathedrals, sports stadiums, airports, bridges, transportation systems, private homes, and people to heaps of smoldering ashes.

For instance, the cities of Seattle and Tacoma, and dozens of smaller towns in the state of Washington—the home of the American aircraft

industry—are located very close to the base of Mount Rainier, a
14,410-foot-high volcano that could erupt tomorrow, killing millions
and burying surrounding populated areas under a mantle of lava and
ash. Mount Rainier is the most dangerous volcano in the United States,
due primarily to the large population nearby and the fact that its upper
slopes carry a load of glacial ice exceeding that of any other mountain
in the lower 48 states. When Mount Rainier erupts—and there is no
question that it will sometime in the future—the plains beneath the
volcano may disappear beneath a flood generated by suddenly melting
glaciers. The deluge could reach as far as Puget Sound, perhaps raising
the water level high enough to flood the port cities of Tacoma and
Seattle.

An eruption of Mount Rainier would also pose several other threats
to the millions of people in the region. Typically, violent eruptions
send up towering columns of hot gases mixed with tephra. When the
mixture reaches an altitude at which the plume can no longer support
the tephra, the volcanic debris begins to drift back to earth, often
covering large areas with layers of ash, pumice, and rock fragments
from several inches to as much as 50 feet deep. Gases ejected from the
volcano—especially carbon monoxide—would also threaten everything
downwind. If the wind happens to be blowing west toward Puget Sound
when Rainier erupts, Tacoma and Seattle would be blanketed with
scalding volcanic debris. Large tephra particles can kill humans on
impact, and many are hot enough to start fires where they land. It is
likely that a large eruption of Mount Rainier would start so many fires
in the surrounding area that tens of thousands of homes and buildings,
plus hundreds of square miles of forest land, would vanish in an unstoppable firestorm. Finer particles can cause respiratory problems, or
even suffocation. Accumulations of tephra can also collapse roof tops,
make highways impassable, ruin crop fields, damage power and telephone lines, and cripple mechanical equipment.

An eruption of Mount Rainier would also produce pyroclastic flows—
mixtures of hot gases and volcanic rock particles—that would race down
the mountain's slopes at speeds up to 200 miles an hour. Pyroclastic
flows are often heated to more than 1,000 degrees Fahrenheit and

incinerate anything in their path. According to the U.S. Geological Survey, debris avalanches and lahars—mixtures of water and sediment that look like flowing concrete—suddenly racing down the slopes of Mount Rainier may pose a terrible threat to the lowlands surrounding the volcano because they can occur without warning.

The largest Mount Rainier lahar that we now know of occurred about 5,600 years ago, and was at least 10 times larger than any other known lahar originating on the volcano. Deposits now cover about 212 square miles in the Puget Sound lowlands, and extend as far as the present sites of Seattle and Tacoma. The USGS also points out that sudden earthquakes, steam explosions, or even heavy rainstorms can trigger debris avalanches that would race down the steep slopes of the volcano and fan out for hundreds of square miles across the plain below. Debris avalanches can also dam up rivers and streams, forming lakes. When the suddenly created lakes exceed their banks, water begins to spill over the earthen barrier before it, eventually bursting through the dam and causing catastrophic floods and lahars. At least six other debris avalanches have created lahars in the Seattle-Tacoma area over the past 5,600 years. One of these, known as the "Electron Mudflow," which occurred a mere 600 years ago, was at least 90 feet deep when it spewed across the Puget Sound lowlands. Today, almost two million people live or work in that area.

Mount Rainier is one of a chain of volcanic peaks that make up the Cascade Range stretching from northern California into Canada. The Cascades are one of the youngest mountain ranges on Earth, and one of the most volcanically active. There are 27 volcanic peaks in the range of towering peaks. In addition to Mount Rainier, the most well known are Mount Hood, Mount Washington, Diamond Peak, Crater Lake, Mount Shasta, Lassen Peak, and the now-infamous Mount St. Helens.

When Mount St. Helens blew apart in a major eruption of magma, ash, and pumice in May 1980, it devastated 212 square miles of land to the south and east of the volcano, killing 57 people, leveling forests, and obliterating all wildlife. The eruption disintegrated the upper 1,300 feet of Mount St. Helens, leaving a crater 2,084 feet deep, 1.8 miles long, and 1.2 miles wide. After the main blast, upwelling magma ejected explosively, sending a towering column of debris and ash 12 miles into the sky, which soon began to rain down on eastern Washington and northern Idaho, reaching populated areas 930 miles from the volcano. Twenty-four square miles of the Toutle Valley were filled to a depth of more than 160 feet by a debris avalanche, 250 square miles of timber-land were flattened by pyroclastic flows, and huge lahars deposited an estimated 200 million cubic yards of material into nearby river channels. In addition to devastating the river systems draining the east and south flanks of the volcano, the lahars carried so much debris into the Columbia River that 31 ships were trapped in upstream ports until the shipping channel could be dredged.

This was devastation on a massive scale. Yet, the death toll caused by the eruption of Mount St. Helens was relatively light compared to many other eruptions in recorded history, primarily because the area was already sparsely populated, and seismic activity within the volcano and a growing bulge on the side of the mountain gave volcanologists several weeks' warning that an eruption was imminent. Authorities were able to evacuate most residents before the volcano blew. Still, the eruption of Mount St. Helens served as a wake-up call for the residents of the Seattle-Tacoma area. Mount Rainier, a volcano that is all but the twin of Mount St. Helens, could blow apart at any time, perhaps in an eruption many times more violent.

Although seismic activity usually precedes an eruption, this is not always the case, and a sudden upwelling of magma within Mount Rainier could doom all life in the Seattle-Tacoma area with little or no warning. Numerous other volcanoes around the world pose the same danger. According to the University of Wisconsin Disaster Management Center, there are approximately 500 active volcanoes on Earth. These deadly mountains are located in Africa, the Southwest Pacific, Southeast Asia, India, Japan, the central Pacific, the American west—particularly the northwest, California, and Alaska—South America, Central America, the Mediterranean area, Iceland, and Antarctica.

Volcanically active areas also include "hot spots," or vents that penetrate tectonic plates like blowtorches burning through solid steel plates. The theory of hot spots was first put forward by Canadian geophysicist

J. Tuzo Wilson in 1963. According to a report from the U.S. Geological Survey, Wilson noted that volcanism had been active for long periods in places such as Hawaii, which is situated in the middle of the huge Pacific plate nowhere near a subduction zone.

FIRE AND WATER

Wilson's explanation was that a thermal plume had risen from the molten interior of the earth, burned through the crust, and over the eons had built up submarine volcanic mountains, which eventually reached the surface of the sea and created the Hawaiian island chain. Because the hot spot is relatively stationary while the Pacific plate—and all other tectonic plates—are in constant motion, the submarine volcanism created one island after another as the Pacific plate drifted northwest over the hot spot.

Evidence that Wilson's theory of hot spots may be correct comes from U.S. Geological Survey studies of the age of the rock formations in the Hawaiian Islands. The USGS has found that, "The oldest volcanic rocks on Kauai, the northwestern most inhabited Hawaiian island, are about 5.5 million years old and are deeply eroded. By comparison, on the Big Island of Hawaii—southeastern-most in the chain and presumably still positioned above the hot spot—the oldest exposed rocks are less than 0.7 million years old and new volcanic rock is continually being formed."

If the vast majority of people were asked the question, "What is the tallest mountain on Earth?" almost everyone would answer "Mount Everest." But this is untrue. The tallest mountain in the world is Mauna Kea in the Hawaiian Islands. From the base of the volcano on the Pacific Ocean floor, Mauna Kea rises 33,476 feet, which is 4,441 feet higher than Mount Everest. Such is the enormous volume of magma being ejected by hot spots.

How much of a danger to the life on Earth—including humanity— do hot spots pose? Scientists now know of more than a hundred hot spots beneath the oceans and continents, and most of these are located under the interior of plates. It is conceivable that you could live in Iowa, the United Kingdom, Germany, or any other region of the world—

areas historically removed from volcanism and earthquakes—and awake tomorrow to find that satellite thermal surveillance has detected a new hot spot that is about to burst through the earth, directly beneath the region where you live or work. Modern satellites equipped with infrared and heat-sensing devices would undoubtedly detect signs of imminent eruptions, and you would probably have enough time to flee to safer areas. But with local or national governments, industries, agriculture, your place of work, and your home obliterated from the face of the earth, how would you carry on?

Yet another threat of life-ending volcanism comes from what are known as rift zones, or spreading centers, where the tectonic plates that make up the earth's crust are pulling apart, allowing molten magma to reach the surface through the fissures that vent the magma rising from below. Perhaps the most widely researched spreading center is the Mid-Atlantic Ridge, a submarine mountain range that extends more than 9,000 miles down the middle of the North and South Atlantic Oceans. In several places, immense eruptions from the ridge have created volcanic seamounts that have risen through the ocean depths to create islands. These include Iceland, the Azores, and St. Helena, among others.

In two previous books, I project a scenario in which a sudden up-welling of magma from the Mid-Atlantic Ridge creates a new island in the North Atlantic, directly in the path of the Gulf Stream, which is a virtual river of warm water from the Gulf of Mexico that runs up the east coast of the United States, and then travels across the Atlantic to warm northern Europe. If such a volcanic event were to occur and the Gulf Stream were diverted from reaching Europe, average temperatures in England, Ireland, the Scandinavian countries, and many other parts of northern Europe would drop as much as 10 degrees Fahrenheit. Equally ominous, if the newly formed volcano spewed enormous quantities of ash and sulfur dioxide into the atmosphere, the volcanic debris and gases could block enough solar radiation to further drop the air temperature over northern Europe, creating sub-Arctic conditions over many countries that today enjoy temperate climates.

Could the Mid-Atlantic Ridge really create a new island in modern times? It already has! In 1963, submarine volcanism off the south coast of Iceland formed the brand-new island of Surtsey. If Surtsey had risen from the black icy depths of the North Atlantic farther south in the path of the Gulf Stream—and was larger in size—it might well have diverted the current of warm water from reaching Europe. The sudden plunge in temperatures from Ireland to Russia would have caused massive agricultural failure, blizzards that paralyzed transportation and commerce, and death from starvation and freezing.

Submarine volcanism can also create tsunamis, or tidal waves, that can inundate surrounding shorelines and flood inland. Tsunamis caused by undersea eruptions are most common in the Pacific, but they have also occurred in the other oceans of the world.

The sudden eruption of island volcanoes can be equally devastating. In 1815, the Indonesian island volcano of Tambora exploded in the largest eruption in modern history. The eruption sent so much ash and gases into the stratosphere that the ejecta formed a huge volcanic cloud that circled the world for several years, blocking out sunlight and lowering the planet's mean temperature by as much as 3 degrees Celsius. The plummeting temperatures and reduced sunlight caused massive crop failures around the world, leading to widespread starvation, and 1815 became known in the United States as "the year without a summer."

Sixty-eight years later, in 1883, a second Indonesian volcano, Krakatau, blew apart, creating a tsunami estimated to have been 115 feet high. The monstrous wave killed tens of thousands of people living along the coasts of Java and Sumatra, destroyed buildings far inland, and was detected more than 8,000 miles across the ocean, reaching shores as far away as Panama in Central America. The eruption of Krakatau also produced one of the loudest noises in history, and was heard more than 3,000 miles away. The titanic explosion sent so much ash, dust, and gas into the upper atmosphere that observers all over the world reported brilliant sunrises and sunsets caused by the refraction of the sun's rays off the tiny particles ejected by the volcano.

One of the most frightening scenarios related to volcanoes is the possibility that submarine and/or subglacial volcanism could erupt in Antarctica—specifically West Antarctica—and that the molten magma and superheated gases surging up under the ice from the fiery bowels of the earth could cause the entire West Antarctic Ice Sheet to slip into the sea and begin to melt.

What are the odds that a volcano could erupt beneath the Antarctic ice? Scientists simply don't know. What is known is that Antarctica is a volcanically active area. The most visible sign of this is 12,444-foot high Mount Erebus on Ross Island in West Antarctica, an active volcano that has been erupting intermittently since 1972. Although it's conceivable that a large eruption of Mount Erebus could melt hundreds of thousands of tons of ice on the volcano's slopes, a far greater threat looms in the existence of unseen submarine and sub-glacial volcanoes. Using radar, seismic probes, and aeromagnetic data, geologists from the U.S. Geological Survey have discovered hundreds of volcanic centers beneath the sea and ice of West Antarctica. Most of these hidden volcanoes are probably inactive. However, it is likely that at least some are active and could erupt at any time.

What concerns scientists is that a violent, prolonged eruption beneath the Ross Ice Shelf—a floating glacier the size of France frozen to the shore of West Antarctica—could break the shelf free of the continent, setting off a chain of events that could lead to catastrophic flooding of the world's seacoasts. The Ross Ice Shelf acts like a cork in a bottle, blocking the seaward movement of the land-bound West Antarctic Ice Sheet. If the shelf melted or broke free of the continent, there would be nothing to restrain the titanic glacier behind it. The entire West Antarctic Ice Sheet could surge forward into the ocean and begin to melt. Scientists estimate that the Ice Sheet contains enough water to raise the earth's sea levels as much as 20 feet. New York, New Orleans, Los Angeles, San Francisco, London, Stockholm, Rio de Janeiro, Hong Kong, Tokyo, and most of the world's other major sea ports would disappear beneath the waves. Millions of square miles of low-lying coastal areas would also be flooded, and several island chains would vanish under the rising seas.

Because the melting of the Ice Sheet—and the subsequent rise in sea level—would be gradual, it is likely that most inhabitants of port cities and coastal regions could be safely evacuated. However, the economic, sociological, and political consequences of such a disaster would result in world-wide chaos and an incalculable number of human deaths.

Without ports—and the loading, unloading, and transportation infra-structures that go with them—the thousands of ships that regularly carry billions of tons of trade goods across the oceans of the world would have no place to dock. The United States could no longer ship the countless tons of wheat, corn, soybeans, meat, and other foodstuffs it now sells abroad. Grain crops would rot in thousands of fields as silos brimmed over, and hundreds of thousands of cattle would have to be destroyed when slaughterhouses and cold storage facilities filled to the rafters with unsold meat. The industrial products of Europe manu-factured for export would overflow warehouses, and millions of cars meant for overseas markets would rust away in makeshift parking lots in Japan. Coffee, tea, bananas, and other tropical-food products would become luxury items in the United States, Europe, and Asia, and with-out direly needed imports of food, starvation would grip many unde-veloped nations, especially in Africa.

The economic upheaval that accompanied the loss of worldwide seaports would make the Great Depression seem like boom times. Hundreds of millions of workers would lose their jobs, and it's doubtful that unemployment systems presently in place could support a rapid influx of such vast hordes of jobless people. In addition to the specter of mass starvation in the undeveloped countries, the industrialized nations would face the loss of fuel imports from the oil-producing countries of the world, especially those in the Persian Gulf area. Without fuel, there would be no gas for cars, no heating oil for homes and busi-nesses, and no natural gas to power our electrical plants. Manufacturing and transportation would come to a screeching halt, and most of the people of the United States, Europe, Asia, and the southern latitudes would have no way to heat their homes during the winters. Countless millions would freeze to death.

Although volcanologists, geologists, and other scientists have studied volcanoes for decades, we still know relatively little about how molten magma feeds up from the planet's fiery interior through the crust, nor can we predict with any assuredness when a volcano will suddenly explode. The only certainty is that a titanic eruption will someday strike the earth—next week, next month, next year—and there's nothing we can do about it.

THE GREENHOUSE EFFECT

Mark Twain once famously observed, "Everybody talks about the weather, but nobody does anything about it." He was wrong. Even in his day, which spanned the latter half of the nineteenth century, the Industrial Revolution had already been going strong for about a century, already laying the groundwork for future climatological changes. People impact the planet. The fires they burn, the crops they raise, the landforms and watercourses they permanently alter, all have a macro effect. For the last two centuries, without knowing it, people *have* been doing something about the weather.

And all along, the weather has been doing something about people. Throughout the ages, floods, droughts, hurricanes and typhoons, monsoons, heat waves, and cold spells all have taken their toll of human casualties. But never before has nature lashed out at humanity with such fury as now, in the age of the superstorm.

To know a fact intellectually is one thing; to know it viscerally is something altogether different. It's the difference between knowing that a punch in the nose hurts and actually being punched in the nose. Humanity had known of the greenhouse effect for some time, but not until the real punishment began was the phenomenon taken seriously.

The world was well on its way up the learning curve as the world's temperate zones became intemperate. In the northern and southern hemispheres, the mid-latitudes were regarded as the temperate zones: not too hot, not too cold, their climates optimal for growing both crops and people. Now, that planetary constant was no more. The mid-latitudes were becoming sultry, semi-tropical, while the equatorial zone was becoming a heat-blasted inferno. Global warming was the culprit—or rather, the symptom. The real culprit was the human race itself.

Industrialization generated the so-called "greenhouse gases": carbon dioxide, water vapor, and such chemical compounds as chlorofluorocarbons. Greenhouse gases, because once airborne they create an effect similar to that of a glass greenhouse: They let the sunlight and heat in, and keep them in. A global heat trap had been created, a self-sustaining mechanism. Solar energy heated the earth. The greenhouse effect contained the heat, causing less of it to dissipate into space. As the temperature rose, increased evaporation of the world's oceans put still more water vapor into the air, increasing the effect.

CHAPTER 4: THE GREENHOUSE EFFECT

The greenhouse effect was a fact conceded even by the administration in Washington, D.C. Instead of trying to limit the production of further such gases, the politicians began drawing up plans to deal with the coming consequences of global warming. As usual, their prognostications and nostrums came too late.

Now, the situation reached a figurative boiling point. Recent years had seen a series of ever-more brutal summers sear the mid-latitudes. Now came the worst yet, one that roasted North America and Europe as never before. From the Canadian border to the Rio Grande, the United States broiled under heat waves in which 105-degree days stretched unbroken into weeks, inflicting devastating economic and human damage.

No power grid could supply the demands made on it by hundreds of millions of air conditioners. Transformer fires were a daily occurrence. Power surges and shortages wreaked havoc on computer systems, crashing entire networks, erasing mountains of data, including bank records, billing departments, and law enforcement criminal files. The most industrialized, electrified section of the country, the urban clusters, were wracked by daily brown-outs and black-outs, the latter often lasting for days and even weeks before total power was restored. Infants, the elderly, and those with respiratory ailments such as emphysema perished in record numbers.

The rural countryside suffered no less badly. The last few independent family farmers who hadn't already been wiped out by hard times and the giant agri-business combines were obliterated by the searing summer heat. Livestock experienced mass die-offs in what had once been pasturelands and were now sun-blasted wastelands.

In the Midwest, the breadbasket of America, drought swallowed up water resources needed to irrigate fields of crops. Corn, wheat, vegetables, and orchards all withered and died under the sun, their millions of square miles of acreage turning into dustbowls. For those dependent on the harvests, the specter of famine loomed imminent.

From California to the eastern seaboard, the forests of America were burning. The sun had turned them into tinderboxes that with the slightest spark turned into raging firestorms consuming thousands of acres. The smoke was clearly visible to astronauts occupying the international space station orbiting the globe.

Further south, what had been the subtropics and the equatorial tropic region were now deserts in progress. Mexico lay parched, its rivers dried up, its greenery sun-blasted into withered brown husks. The rainforests of Central America and the islands of the Caribbean were brown, bone-dry—and burning.

For the past few years, the press of refugees trying to escape starvation by fleeing north to the United States had caused National Guard troops to police key crossing points. Now, the imperatives of survival had forced huddled masses to swarm the sites, held back at the point of bayonets and machine guns, causing daily scenes of heartbreaking human tragedy.

Worse lay ahead, as the season of the superstorm dawned. In northern latitudes, mid-summer through early fall had always been prime hurricane season. Now, global warming had turned up the flame on the hurricanes that bloomed in the Caribbean Sea, energizing the cyclonic storm-patterns that formed in the region. As August yielded to September, a series of hurricanes slammed the Caribbean, Gulf Coast, and southeastern United States. Devastating though they were, all signs indicated that the burgeoning Hurricane Daria would be a storm to make the others look tame. A massive, furious storm system, it pulverized the islands with nonstop 120-mile-per-hour winds and massive flooding. The deluge killed thousands, with scores of thousands subsequently dying from the plague generated by so many bloated, floating corpses.

Charging north, Daria hit Florida head on, mauling it from Key West to Jacksonville. The vortex tossed uprooted trees and telephone poles like jackstraws, turning them into unguided missiles that ripped through town and country. Unabated, the storm charged northeast, rolling through Georgia like a gale-force General Sherman. Daria steamrolled up the eastern seaboard, hammering the coastal regions all the way to Boston before careening out to the North Atlantic and finally dissipating. Thousands were dead and injured; hundreds of thousands were homeless.

Daria was the storm of the century, the biggest storm of all time. So said the news media, after patching together their storm-battered infrastructure. The storm of the century, that is, until three weeks later, when Hurricane Gunther came roaring north, inflicting damage which made Daria look tame.

The era of the superstorm had arrived, spawned by global warming. After a lukewarm, soupy winter, the next year's late winter and early spring saw the advent of a second type of superstorm. Coming out of the north, the front of heavy rain spanned the nation from coast to coast, piling up masses of mile-high clouds, writhing and roiling. The tempest broke, loosing seemingly inexhaustible torrents of rain. It rained for days and days, accompanied by gale-force winds. Hardest hit was the Midwest, but no low-lying region west or east was spared from being flooded by the deluge.

The polar melting that had begun years before now accelerated, causing a significant rise in the sea level whose unprecedented force and speed would begin drowning coastal cities within a decade.

But that lay ahead. As the northern hemisphere lurched into what scientists predicted would be the hottest summer yet, Canadian authorities were quietly fortifying key crossing points on their border with the United States, in anticipation of hordes of Americans trying to escape their steaming hell for the relatively temperate Canadian northlands.

———————————————— ■ ————————————————

Within decades—perhaps even years—a human-made hell will descend upon the earth. Searing temperatures and droughts will lead to widespread crop failures and mass starvation. As the climate grows warmer, diseases will reach pandemic proportions and storms will triple in intensity. The earth's rising temperatures will melt the polar ice caps and the seas will begin to rise, flooding ports and cutting off shipments of oil and natural gas. As supplies of home heating oil disappear, millions of people in the higher latitudes will freeze to death during the winter, while the lack of fuel to power factories and vehicles will cripple worldwide industry and bring transportation to a halt. Commerce in the United States and abroad will cease to function, and billions will lose their jobs. Billions more will be forced to flee from their homes as the rising seas flood far inland. As hordes of starving, homeless people search desperately for sustenance and shelter, society will inevitably disintegrate into a lawless struggle for survival.

The architect of this Armageddon is neither fate nor the forces of nature, but humans themselves. There is growing evidence that human activities—especially the burning of fossil fuels, the felling of forests, and the widespread use of fertilizers—are profoundly changing the climate of the earth, trapping solar energy that would normally escape into space and raising surface temperatures precipitously.

The earth's atmosphere is composed of 78 percent nitrogen, 21 percent oxygen, 1 percent argon, and a fraction of a percent of greenhouse gases, which either occur naturally or are made by humans. These gases consist primarily of water vapor, followed by carbon dioxide, methane, nitrous oxide, and manufactured chemicals such as chlorofluorocarbons. Greenhouse gases derive their name from the fact that they trap heat in the lower atmosphere, much like the glass of a greenhouse that lets the sun's rays in but prevents the warmth from escaping.

Although greenhouse gases make up only a tiny percentage of the atmosphere, they play an indispensable role in regulating the climate of our planet. Without these gases, a far greater percentage of the heat energy the earth receives from the sun would be reflected back into space. Scientists calculate that if there were no greenhouse gases in the atmosphere, the mean temperature of our planet would plunge to about two degrees Fahrenheit instead of today's average surface temperature of 59 degrees Fahrenheit. Very few of the world's present life forms, including the human species, could exist under such conditions.

To get an idea of how important the greenhouse gases are to life on earth, we need only look at our two neighboring planets, Mars and Venus. Because Mars has a rarefied atmosphere containing low concentrations of greenhouse gases, most of the solar energy radiates back into space, leaving the planet's surface too cold to sustain life. The opposite is true of Venus, which has an atmosphere saturated with such high concentrations of carbon dioxide that the gas prevents radiant heat from escaping back out through the atmosphere. The result is surface temperatures that average near 900 degrees Fahrenheit, far too hot to allow life as we know it to survive.

Yet even though greenhouse gases have nurtured life on earth for billions of years, they also have the potential to kill off every plant and animal species on the planet if their volume continues to grow unchecked. Unfortunately, unless humanity radically changes its ways, this is exactly what will happen. Several years ago, Greenpeace polled 400 international climatologists and found that 45 percent of those who responded believed that a runaway greenhouse effect—a point of no return beyond which lay unstoppable heating of the planet—was possible.

GAS HEAT

We are pouring more carbon dioxide into the atmosphere than the earth's natural mechanisms, such as the absorption of carbon dioxide by trees and plants, can process. The result has been a steady rise in atmospheric carbon dioxide levels ever since the Industrial Revolution began 250 years ago. The more carbon dioxide in the atmosphere, the greater the effect on the earth's heat balance. The Intergovernmental Panel on Climate Change (IPCC), a United Nations task force studying our climate, has projected a "mid-range" temperature rise of 2 to 5 degrees Fahrenheit by the end of the century, and many climatologists believe that temperatures could go up by more than 10 degrees Fahrenheit. Most scientists now agree that the greenhouse effect is inexorably propelling the earth toward the edge of a climatic cliff, beyond which lies an abyss of death and destruction.

To be sure, there are well-respected scientists who discount the possibility of catastrophic climatic changes. They point out that natural processes such as volcanic eruptions, animal respiration, and the decay of organic material has been releasing carbon dioxide into the air for eons. It is also true that methane is produced when substances containing carbon decompose and when natural microorganisms in damp soil break down organic matter. The earth has always had natural processes to remove greenhouse gases from the atmosphere. Oceans and lakes absorb carbon dioxide from the air, and plants draw in the gas during photosynthesis to use in making food. There is also indisputable evidence that our climates have gone through both gradual and sudden temperature changes—either warming or cooling—innumerable times in history, and that some temperature rises have been as steep as that which models predict will occur as a result of a heightened greenhouse effect.

Scientists who downplay humanity's role in the burgeoning greenhouse effect fail to take several key factors into account.

All this is true. Yet scientists who downplay humanity's role in the burgeoning greenhouse effect, while unquestionably sincere, fail to take several key factors into account. For instance, while it is true that volcanic eruptions and the breakdown of organic material produce huge quantities of carbon dioxide and methane, many other natural processes like plant photosynthesis and absorption by the oceans draw carbon dioxide from the air. Each year, nature adds and removes approximately the same amount of carbon from the atmosphere, maintaining a balance of greenhouse gases. This natural balance is upset when man "enhances" the greenhouse effect by burning fossil fuels, felling forests, and releasing manufactured chemicals into the atmosphere.

Other greenhouse gases produced by humans are less common than carbon dioxide, but pound-for-pound have a far greater effect on the atmosphere. Nitrous oxide is some 300 times as effective as carbon dioxide at trapping heat. Although carbon dioxide is a thousand times more prevalent, nitrous oxide remains in the atmosphere far longer, adding to the greenhouse effect for a century or more.

Chlorofluorocarbons and other fluorinated compounds, which do not occur in nature and can only be produced by humans, trap up to 13,000 times more heat than carbon dioxide, and can remain in the atmosphere for as long as 400 years. Chlorofluorocarbons are particularly sinister because, when they reach the upper atmosphere, sunlight breaks the compounds down, releasing chlorine. Each chlorine atom can destroy up to 100,000 ozone molecules. Since the ozone layer protects life on Earth from lethal exposure to the sun's cancer-causing ultraviolet radiation, chlorofluorocarbons present a duel threat to both humans and animals. Excessive exposure to a type of ultraviolet light called UV-B can also damage crops and the marine food chain.

Scientists believe that a recently discovered hole that appears periodically in the ozone layer over Antarctica is caused by a concentration of chlorofluorocarbons in the atmosphere of the southern hemisphere. The ozone layer in other regions of the world is also being decimated by chlorofluorocarbons. For several days during the winter of 1995–1996, the World Meteorological Organization observed up to a 25 percent depletion of the ozone layer over a vast area of the northern hemisphere, stretching from Greenland across Europe to Siberia.

According to an article in the *Encarta Encyclopedia* titled "Greenhouse Effect," experts are increasingly concerned about other industrial chemicals that may have heat-trapping abilities. "In 2000, scientists observed rising concentrations of a previously unreported compound called trifluoremethyl sulphur pentafluoride," the article reports. The danger this gas presents is that it traps heat in the lower atmosphere far more efficiently than all other greenhouse gases presently known.

Despite findings that prove that carbon dioxide, methane, nitrous oxide, and synthetic chemicals are humanity's most harmful additions to greenhouse gases, other research indicates that we have even managed to heighten the negative impact of a substance as benign as water vapor. Water vapor is the most prevalent of the greenhouse gases and is responsible for 60 to 70 percent of the natural greenhouse effect. Although humans do not have a great influence on water-vapor levels, our introduction of other gases into the atmosphere warms the earth and leads to greater evaporation from oceans and lakes. Computer projections also predict that a warmer climate will bring an increase in rainfall in both hemispheres, especially during the winter months. Torrential downpours and blizzards will become more common, and catastrophic floods will inevitably follow in their wake.

HORRORS OF A WARMER WORLD

Clearly, ever since the start of the Industrial Revolution 250 years ago, human activities have increasingly worsened the greenhouse effect, upsetting the balance of nature and leading directly to the present artificial and precipitous warming of the earth. Humans are to blame for the catastrophic climate changes hovering just over the horizon, yet our species is not the only life form that will suffer and struggle to survive through the terrible times to come. Aquatic plants and animals will be especially vulnerable to our changing climate. Plankton, the first rung on the aquatic food ladder, will be severely impacted as the greenhouse effect worsens. As plankton begins to disappear from the seas, so will hundreds of species of fish and crustaceans higher up the food chain. Cod, salmon, halibut, tuna, anchovies, shrimp, crabs, lobsters, and countless other marine species will become severely depleted or even go extinct, and indigenous populations around the world who depend on the sea for food will face starvation.

The greenhouse effect will heat up the oceans, lakes, and rivers to the point where they will become too warm for many species of aquatic life to survive. Billions of dead fish and crustaceans will carpet every shore, each rotting corpse an incubator for insects and disease. Those species of marine plants and animals that survive the decimation of plankton and the steadily warming seas and lakes will face a problematic fate, as the rising temperatures suck more and more oxygen from the water.

Birds would also be highly vulnerable to sudden climatic change, especially if the warmer air and sea start to melt the polar ice caps and the oceans begin to rise. A recent position paper on the greenhouse effect from Penn State University warns, "Global warming has both direct and indirect effects on birds. Higher temperatures can directly alter their life cycles. The loss of wetlands, beaches, and other habitat has an indirect effect on birds by making some regions less hospitable to birds."

Beyond missing the trill of birds calling at dawn, the colorful company of a canary in a cage, or the stirring sight of a flock of migrating geese gracefully cutting through the sky, should we be concerned about the imminent plight of birds? Yes, and for reasons far beyond the aesthetic. Birds carry thousands of varieties of seeds from place to place, transplanting trees and plants to new areas where they can flourish. Even if we employed every technological and horticultural innovation available today, humans could not possibly duplicate the ability of birds to distribute seeds and pollen across the earth and rejuvenate plant life. In addition, birds and their eggs are also a vital food source for scores of wild carnivores such as foxes, cougars, reptiles, fish, spiders, and over a hundred other predators, including humans. If a sudden greenhouse warming of the planet kills off a large number of bird species, our entire ecosystem will go into shock, and ultimately thousands of other species of both plants and animals will perish.

As our climate continues to grow hotter, the populations of insects native to the temperate regions will explode, and new species of bugs will move north from the tropics (see Chapter 9). Birds consume countless trillions of insects each year, keeping insect species in balance with the rest of nature. If the number of birds on earth decreases drastically, hordes of mosquitoes, flies, cockroaches, scorpions, ants, bees, wasps, and masses of other insects will swarm into our homes and workplaces. In the United States and the other industrialized nations, those who must work outdoors will suffer the most. Farmers, ranchers, migrant workers, construction crews, policemen, and legions of other workers will have to wear protective clothing and netting over their faces. From America to Europe, Russia, China, and Japan, doors will have to be kept tightly shut to keep out hordes of bugs no matter how hot it gets during the summer months.

Swarms of locusts will likely move north from their normal range near the equator to devour crops in regions of the Americas, Europe, and Asia where they have never been seen before. Along with the locusts will come other insects native to the tropics, inflicting food shortages, diseases, and poisonous bites on the humans in their path. In the poverty-stricken third-world countries of Central and South America, Africa, and Asia, the infestation of insects caused by the greenhouse effect will endanger entire populations. With the air and ground saturated with swarming hordes of bugs, people will no longer be able to venture outside to tend their crops, herd their livestock, or gather food in the forest. Commerce between villages and towns will become impossible as insects clog carburetors and drive pack animals mad. The straw huts, windowless shanties, and wall-less shelters that are the main source of housing in the tropics will provide no protection from the hordes of voracious insects that will descend on the equatorial regions. Clouds of mosquitoes will fill the air, swarms of flies will cover every scrap of food, and killer bees, wasps, army ants, and scorpions will sting hundreds of thousands of people to death.

According to a study titled *Global Warming, Early Warning Signs* compiled by a group of organizations including the Environmental Defense Fund, the Sierra Club, and the World Resources Institute, "Warmer temperatures allow mosquitoes that transmit diseases such as malaria and dengue fever to extend their biting rate and their ability to infect humans."

And insects are not the only vermin that will flourish if the birds die off. The rodent population of the planet—with one of the highest reproduction rates of any mammal—will skyrocket overnight. Tens of billions of rats and mice will descend upon grain fields and silos in the Americas, Europe, Africa, Asia, and Australia, devouring entire harvests and spoiling millions more tons of grain with their droppings. The voracious vermin will gnaw off the teats of milk cows and nursing horses, sheep, goats, and pigs. They will tear newborn poultry chicks to pieces while still alive, and suck dry billions of eggs. In residential areas and cities, hordes of rodents will find their way into every kitchen and cupboard, devouring cereal, sugar, flour, and other dry foods. They will eat the insulation off electrical wiring in search of salt, shorting out circuits, plunging homes into darkness and cold, and starting fires. The rodents—tens of millions of them covered with infected fleas— will spread disease throughout entire countries and continents. Doctors and hospitals will be overwhelmed by the epidemic, and unable to provide sufficient care to all. The young, the old, and the sick will die first. Without winged predators to thin their ranks, reptile populations will also swell beyond human control.

Sudden global warming will also devastate scores of other life forms. As weather patterns inevitably change, now-lush grasslands will become dust bowls. Millions of wild grazing animals such as deer, elk, antelope, and buffalo will likely starve to death, as will the predators that depend on these animals for food. Forests all over the world will also begin dying out as the changing climate alters rain patterns and the length of seasons. Both coniferous evergreens and broad-leafed species such as oak, elm, maple, and chestnut trees will not survive for long in the throes of a major climatic upheaval.

Dryland and wetland plant species alike will be unable to adapt to the rapidly changing climate, and the stricken flora of the earth will cloak prairies, forest floors, and swamps with blankets of rotting vegetation. As trees and plants die out, so will the legions of animals that survive by eating nuts, seeds, fruits, leaves, shoots, and bark. With no food to be found in the forests, fields, and prairies, the surviving wildlife will have no choice but to invade human habitats in a desperate search for sustenance. Herbivores like deer and rabbits will overrun suburban areas, eating every shrub and blade of grass they can find. Wild carnivores like mountain lions, wolves, and coyotes will follow, and when they cannot find their natural prey, they will turn to devouring domestic cats and dogs. The starving meat-eaters will threaten humans as well. With voracious predators roaming residential areas, no woman will dare risk pruning the rose bushes or sunbathing outside, no man will be secure mowing the lawn or shoveling snow, and no child will be safe walking home from school or playing in the backyard.

WHAT HAVE WE DONE? WHAT CAN WE DO?

How do futurists know that this scary scenario will actually come true? Because it has already begun. Humanity's rapacious exploitation of the earth's resources has been wreaking havoc on our planet's ecosystems for centuries. Humans have impacted and altered our ecosystems—from our forests to our polar regions to our savannahs to our seas—so profoundly and irreversibly that we have crippled the ability of countless species of flora and fauna to survive the worsening greenhouse effect. Trees, plants, and grasses that once flourished across continents have been reduced to scattered pockets of vegetation that are highly susceptible to any temperature change. Windblown pollution and acid rain threaten even these survivors. Every day, thousands of acres of wild habitat—home to hundreds of plant and animal species—disappear beneath new subdivisions, parking lots, shopping malls, and highways. Forests are felled to construct houses that could easily be built of other materials; estuaries critical to marine and bird life are filled in to raise ocean-front condos; and prairies are plowed under by huge corporate farms in an unceasing effort to coax ever more crops from the ground with chemical fertilizers that pollute our air and water.

Rivers are dammed to meet electric power needs that could be reduced by conservation, and to supply water to keep golf courses and private lawns green in the midst of deserts where nature never intended grass to grow. The dams block the millennia-old migration of salmon and other fish, preventing their natural life cycles and cutting off a vital food source for bears, birds, and other wildlife upstream. These towering concrete corks also form immense artificial lakes that flood meadowlands and forests, destroying the habitats of hundreds of species. Wildlife that have drawn their sustenance from pristine pastures and virgin forests now exist by raiding domesticated herds of sheep and cattle, crop fields, garbage dumps, and backyards. As land animals are driven from their natural feeding grounds, waterfowl and fish weaken their immune systems by ingesting aquatic plants, plankton, and small crustaceans poisoned by pollution.

Humans have set the stage for the greenhouse effect to deal the death blow to tens of thousands of species of plants and animals, and the bell will soon chime. As certain as the sun rises and sets, humanity will hear the peal of doom as well. The *Global Warming* report warns that, "Frequent and severe heat waves lead to increases in heat-related illness and death, especially in urban areas and among the elderly, the young, the ill, and the poor."

Research by scientists at Penn State University has found that, "Severe temperatures may be the cause of the loss of life for some people. A number of extreme diseases have been found to appear within warm climates. The increase in temperature (also) affects air and water pollution, which have a direct impact on human health.

"Climate change may cause people to die for various (other) reasons as a result of hotter temperatures. Some people will put pressure on their heart because their cardiovascular system must work harder to keep them cool. They may suffer from respiratory problems or from heat exhaustion."

Eric Chivian and Paul R. Epstein, directors of the Center for Health and the Global Environment at Harvard Medical School, also believe that a hotter climate will lead to an outbreak of disease, respiratory problems, and heat-related deaths. "Illness and death may result from increasing levels of air pollution, exacerbated by the warming, affecting those with chronic respiratory diseases, such as children with asthma and the elderly with bronchitis and emphysema."

The earth's steadily warming climate will produce summers that are unbearably hot. A warning sign came in July 1995, when a prolonged heat wave struck Chicago, killing more than 700 people. As the temperature rose to over 100 degrees, the city's funeral homes were overwhelmed, and additional gravediggers had to be hired to bury the dead.

Humankind is also now faced with the chilling scenario that the greenhouse effect will cause widespread outbreaks of insect-borne diseases. If, as many scientists now predict, the greenhouse effect causes warmer winters and wetter springs, this will greatly enhance breeding conditions for many species of insects, including disease-carrying mosquitoes and ticks. As temperatures rise in the more northerly latitudes, mosquitoes that transmit malaria will be able to extend both their range and their reproduction rate. As the mosquitoes mount their northern invasion, other vector-borne diseases likely to spread beyond the tropics include dengue fever, yellow fever, and encephalitis.

The greenhouse effect will change our weather in other ways as well. As the greenhouse effect grows ever more severe, we can expect that the number of weather related deaths will mushroom as floods inundate entire cities and blizzards rage through ever harsher winters. The *Global Warming* report predicts that, "A warmer climate will bring an increase in precipitation worldwide, especially during winter, according to climate model projections. In addition, more precipitation is expected to fall in downpours and heavy snowstorms, leading to increased flooding and damages. The area of the United States affected by extreme rainfall has increased significantly since 1910. Heavy rainfalls have also increased in Japan, the former Soviet Union, China, and Australia."

Paradoxically, while large areas of the earth experience increased precipitation, other regions will suffer through extended droughts. Wildfires will scorch the land, parched crops will wither in the fields, and trees will become vulnerable to pest infestations and disease. Along with catastrophic floods, blizzards, and droughts, as the greenhouse effect grows increasingly severe, more water will evaporate from the surface of the earth, fueling the heat engine that drives the weather and intensifying storms.

Catherine Senior of Britain's Meteorological Office in Bracken, who has been studying the likely effects of global warming on storms in the middle latitudes, says, "Water vapor is a great energy source. By evaporating more water, we're sucking energy out of the oceans and dumping it into the atmosphere where it's free to do its worst."

A computer model created by Senior strongly suggests that water vapor has a profound influence on our weather, and that global warming will almost surely intensify mid-latitude storms.

There are already warning signals that more severe storms are forming in the North Atlantic and threatening the eastern seaboard of the United States. Ulrich Cusbasch, a scientist at the German Institute for Climate Research in Hamburg, has discovered that, in the past 20 years, mid-Atlantic depressions have worsened, creating more intense storms. As the winds become ever stronger, increasingly severe tornadoes and thunderstorms will wreak havoc in the interior of the continents, while hurricanes in the Atlantic and cyclones in the Pacific ravish the seashores, destroying homes and human lives.

Can such a scary scenario actually occur? We have only to look at the recent meteorological record to find the answer. According to an article in the British magazine *New Scientist* by Gabrielle Walker, the seven warmest years on record occurred during the 1990s, and 1998 was the hottest of all.

"It was the warmest year in the warmest decade in the warmest century in the millennium," says Phil Jones, joint director of the University of East Anglia's Climate Research Unit in Norwich, England.

As the heat engine that drives the weather continued to gain momentum through the 1990s, the weather of the earth changed in dramatic and unprecedented ways that portend calamitous times ahead. Walker adds this about our current weather. "An unruly beast at the best of times, it now seems to be lurching out of control. There are wildfires raging across the western United States. India is reeling from floods that (have) left hundreds dead and millions homeless. Then there's the blistering heat wave in Greece, a bizarre contrast with Yorkshire's recent spectacular hailstorm, which left the streets of Hull looking for all the world as if it had snowed in August."

Walker goes on to note that, "Tropical storms have been more catastrophic in recent years—in both human and economic cost. Hurricane Mitch, for instance, tore through Nicaragua and Honduras in 1998, causing more than 9,000 deaths."

As our climate continues to warm, yet another weather phenomenon known as El Niño—a periodic warming of the eastern Pacific—has been wreaking havoc on nations from Australia to the United States. Normally, the trade winds blow east to west, piling up warm surface water in the seas off Indonesia. But during El Niño cycles, the trade winds weaken, allowing warm water to move east toward the Americas.

Because warmer ocean temperatures contribute directly to rainfall, the shifting of warm water from the west to the east Pacific leaves Indonesia, Australia, and adjacent lands on the Asian side of the Pacific dry and vulnerable to devastating wildfires. At the same time, sudden floods and mudslides plague North and South America.

The geological records indicate that for millennia, El Niños have occurred every six or seven years. But during the past quarter-century—as the greenhouse effect became ever stronger—El Niños have been appearing at two- to three-year intervals. Researcher Fred Pearce writes in *New Scientist*, "Until recently, climatologists looked on El Niño as an aberration in the tropical Pacific of only passing interest to the outside world. But in the past two decades it has become the fifth horseman of the Apocalypse, a bringer of devastating floods, fires, and famine from Ethiopia to Indonesia to Ecuador, and a sender of weird weather around the world."

Famine is an all but certain consequence of the worsening greenhouse effect. The UN Environment Programme (UNEP) recently issued a stark warning of what global warming could do: "Harvests of vital crops like rice, wheat, and corn could plummet by a third over the next 100 years, leaving billions to starve."

The UNEP study cites alarming studies by the International Rice Research Institute in Manila showing that crop yields can drop by 10 percent for every 1.8 degree-Fahrenheit rise in the earth's surface temperatures. Because scientists are predicting a future global warming of up to 10 degrees Fahrenheit, we could be facing a loss of almost 50 percent of the world's rice crop. The entire populations of scores of countries—mostly in Asia—depend on rice to survive. If the greenhouse effect wipes out half the rice harvest for decades or centuries to come, starvation is inevitable.

An equally dire threat posed by the greenhouse effect is the certainty of rising sea levels. As surface and air temperatures heat up, the polar ice caps will melt and the oceans will begin to swell. In a *Worldwatch News Brief*, science writer Lisa Mastny notes that, "The earth's ice cover is melting in more places and at higher rates than at any time since record-keeping began. Reports from around the world compiled by the Worldwatch Institute show that global ice melting accelerated during the 1990s—which was also the warmest decade on record."

Ice sheets and glaciers are melting in both the Arctic and Antarctic regions. The Greenland Ice Sheet, which contains approximately 8 percent of the world's ice, is steadily shrinking, and in Antarctica, which holds 90 percent of the planet's ice, massive sections of floating ice shelves are breaking free of the continent and drifting out to melt in the southern oceans.

In early 2002, the University of Colorado's National Snow and Ice Data Center (NSIDC) reported that a large section of the Larsen Ice Shelf, a huge, floating ice mass on the eastern side of the Antarctic Peninsula, had broken away from the continent. The section of ice shelf that broke free of the Antarctic continent totaled more than 3,250 square kilometers—larger than the state of Rhode Island. Although the flotilla of icebergs produced by the partial collapse of the Larsen Ice Shelf will likely endanger shipping—and even impact local weather—in the lower latitudes of the southern hemisphere for some time, a greater threat looms in the possibility that the immense land-based ice sheets in Antarctica will begin to melt. If this happens, sea levels around the world will rise, inundating our large port cities.

Along with the flooding of our seaports, scientists predict that the homes of an astounding half of the world's population will disappear beneath the waves, as will millions of square miles of rich agricultural land on every continent. An editorial in *New Scientist* contends that, "We have probably already signed death warrants for several low-lying Pacific islands, casualties of rising sea levels."

What can be done to reign in global warming? An article in *Cambridge Scientific Abstracts* by Heather E. Lindsay concludes that, "Putting the brakes on global warming is no easy matter." Lindsay recommends that we begin to reduce greenhouse gases by setting strict emissions standards, cutting down on the use of fossil fuels, developing nonpolluting alternative sources of energy, stopping the use of chlorofluorocarbons, and slowing down deforestation, among other measures.

On the positive side, governments worldwide have now recognized the terrible threat to life as we know it posed by the greenhouse effect, and there is an ongoing international effort to drastically curtail humanity's pollution of our atmosphere. In 1997, representatives of more than 170 nations gathered in Kyoto, Japan, to sign the Kyoto Protocol, an agreement to limit future greenhouse gas emissions. The signatories included the United States, the countries of the European Union, Canada, and Japan.

The agreement suffered a serious setback, however, when the U.S. Senate, in a 95–0 vote, declared that it would not ratify the treaty unless large developing nations such as China, India, and Brazil make a commitment to reduce their significant greenhouse emissions. The primary U.S. concern, however, was that the strict emissions limitations the protocol called for would severely hamper American industry. Despite a campaign pledge to reduce carbon dioxide emissions from U.S. power plants, President Bush—a former Texas oilman—has expressed doubts about the science behind global warming forecasts and renounced the protocol as being too costly to the American economy. On March 28, 2001, Christie Todd Whitman, head of the Environmental Protection Agency, told reporters, "We have no interest in implementing that treaty." An article published by the Environment News Service that same day reported, "Whitman's statement today is the clearest indication yet that U.S. involvement in United Nations organized climate change talks is all but over."

While many other countries—including the G8, a group consisting of the world's eight largest industrialized nations—support the treaty, there continues to be widespread disagreement about how the industrialized countries should be allowed to meet their emission reduction targets. As a result of all this squabbling and the reluctance of Bush Administration to sign the accord, the Kyoto Protocol has never taken full effect, and the nations of the world continue to spew an ever-increasing volume of pollutants into the atmosphere. Many of those politicians arguing against radical environmental reform truly believe that scientists are overstating the seriousness of the greenhouse effect. They insist that more research must be done before we hobble industry to clean up our atmosphere.

Measured against this view, in an article entitled *Sudden Climate Change Through Human History*, science writers Jonathan Adams and Randy Foote caution us to be skeptical of those who downplay the mounting threat of the greenhouse effect. "Gradualist arguments have assumed that humanity could adapt to the effects of slow global warming, with the associated rising of sea levels and changes in agricultural growing patterns. It is likely, though, that Earth's climate does not change in such gentle rhythms. A better model than the gradualist one might be plate tectonics, in which stress generally surfaces in the form of earthquakes, rather than gradual motion and shifting."

We know from the geologic record that past cataclysmic events have wiped out up to 90 percent of all the life forms on Earth. Sixty-five million years ago, an asteroid impact killed off the dinosaurs. Human beings have established wondrous civilizations, nourished the enlightened concepts of democracy and freedom, invented incredible technologies, and explored the farthest reaches of space. Yet humans will never be a match for nature, and if we do not come to recognize that we are poisoning our planet's environment—and the human race with it—we will vanish into time as surely as the dinosaurs and the other species that once dominated the earth.

THE COMING ICE AGE

2010 C.E.

A real old-fashioned winter, complete with cold, ice, and snow, had been largely absent from the world for the past decade, if not longer. The greenhouse effect was responsible for a global warming trend. That was the generally accepted theory—upsetting enough, if you thought about it—but most people managed to ignore it.

Then came the winter of 2010. The summer preceding it had been unusually cool, more like autumn. Rare sunny days turned cool quickly after the sun went down. Mostly it was rainy or overcast and chilly, except for about 10 hot days in August. It was a prelude to glaciation—but nobody knew it at the time, not even the scientists.

Fall came early that year in most parts of the United States. With it came record killing frosts and cold spells, stabbing down deep into the southland, destroying much of Georgia's and Florida's fruit crops. Before the growers could place their smudge pots in the groves, the vast acres of orchards lay buried beneath an icy white crust.

In mid-November, a monster cold front descended from the north, blanketing much of the United States in sub-freezing temperatures, locking the upper half of the nation in a deep-freeze. Retailers warmed themselves with all the extra sales they were ringing up in coats and jackets, scarves, gloves, sweaters, thermal underwear, thick woolen socks, and every other warm garment in stock.

The massive cold front remained in place. Beyond it, in Arctic regions far to the north, things were happening. Sub-storms brewed, whirling, reeling in a sea of clouds. Its titanic energies astir, the conglomerate superstorm lurched forward, sliding southward into Canada, shedding snow all along the way.

In the upper half of the United States, the cold spell eased its grip, succeeded by a few deceptively mild days. In the stores, the merchants uneasily eyed the masses of extra inventory they'd stockpiled in anticipation of a big winter. Now it was shaping up like other recent winters—not so much a time of ice and snow as a rainy season.

For a day or two, Americans watched with indifference, then growing interest, the media coverage of the snowstorm that had paralyzed Canada.

Then it hit the United States. When the advancing front edged the belt of warmer air, it set off a multi-state line of violent thunderstorms. Purple lightning flashing under heavy, charcoal-gray clouds.

The storm actually was not one but many storms. On Thanksgiving Day, the northeast found itself under 18 inches of snow—more than had fallen in the last five years combined. Yet it was only the opening gun of a bombardment of storms that now successively battered the northern, midwestern, and central states. More snow fell on December 7, causing those in its path to recall the meaning of the word *blizzard*. Any novelty that the return of icy weather might have held was by now exhausted for all but the young; they got to stay out of school. For everybody else, the snow was a hardship.

The snow on the ground never had a chance to melt before the next storm piled on more, and the next, and the next. Some 10 full-blown blizzards blitzed the United States that winter. It was expensive, costing businesses thousands of workhours and draining the treasuries of local and state governments forced to deal with it.

Spring came late, with snowfalls of up to 12 inches occurring deep into April. When the last of the white stuff had melted away, most people agreed that if that was a real, old-fashioned winter, bring on global warming.

2015 C.E.

Five years later, the reality was undeniable: the earth *was* getting colder. The cooling trend was an accomplished fact. Hardest hit by the climatic change was the northern hemisphere.

Already, the last five years of savage, stormy winters had caused a decline in the living standards of most of the industrialized world, largely located in the north. Colder weather created greater demand for heating oil, driving up prices and causing shortages, hoarding, black markets. The oil-producing nations charged all the market could bear, increasing global tensions that inevitably exploded into coups, riots, and war.

Winter weather took its toll on the American infrastructure. Roofs buckled and collapsed under the weight of snow. Corrosion from the massive amounts of salt on icy streets damaged roadways, and then seeped below to leach away at underground conduits and cables. Pipes froze and burst, depriving homes of running water. The melted snow generally was unhealthy to drink, contaminated as it was by airborne pollutants.

Ice storms turned cities and suburbs into crystalline wonderlands. The lovely but weighty iceworks dragged down overhead phone lines and power cables, causing communications and power blackouts.

The United States, knit together by its transportation web, now began to unravel. Storms and icing kept planes grounded more often than not. Railroads were buried under new snow faster than plows could clear the tracks. Town and country were isolated, making it harder for farmers to bring their produce to market. Not that there was much left to market. Sudden storms left thousands of head of prime livestock frozen to death throughout the farm belt. The hemisphere—the world—was suffering from a food shortage of epidemic proportions, a fast-galloping famine.

Food distribution is based on trucks bringing farm produce to the urban centers. When the trucks can't get through, cities run out of food fast. How much food does the average apartment dweller or family have stockpiled away? A week? A month at the most? And when that runs out, what then?

It was also, paradoxically, a time of fire. When furnaces went cold, most people didn't just sit there waiting to freeze to death. They built fires. Sometimes they accidentally burned up themselves, their homes, and the homes of those around them, whole city blocks. Water for fire hoses was frequently unavailable: frozen underground, or trickling out of broken mains.

The global warming trend had reversed itself; the planet was no longer warming up but was instead cooling down. Why?

It was the astronomers who came up with the answer. They'd taken their cue from Milankovitch, the Serbian astronomer who'd postulated that variations in Earth's orbit directly affect the advance and retreat of ice ages. Eon after eon, the earth revolved around the sun in endless orbits, ticking away like a cosmic clock, but subject to small but distinct variations of position. It was a matter of eccentricity, axial tilt, and precession, the savants said. What it meant was that on this turn of the cosmic round, a combination of variables had interacted to deprive the earth of a significant amount of solar radiation. Solar radiation fell more evenly on the equator and high latitudes, causing cooler summers and warmer winters. This was optimum for creating a new ice age. Warmer winters put more moisture in the air, which fell as snow at the poles; cooler summers caused less ice to melt, allowing the polar ice caps to expand.

Five years earlier, although no one had known it at the time, the tipping point had been reached. The summer was cool, but winter turned colder. The ice age mechanism had reached its self-sustaining critical threshold, turning down the thermostat on planet Earth.

2035 C.E.

Like a conveyor belt flying loose from its bearings, the Gulf Stream had shuddered and jarred to a halt, immobilized by desalinization. Lacking its life giving warmth, Europe froze. As the global ice caps expanded, covering more of the earth's surface, the white snow and ice reflected more sunlight back into space, causing the earth to grow colder still.

Twenty years later, in the year 2035, the northern hemisphere was frozen tight, a lifeless polar wasteland, abandoned even by the caribou who had migrated down from Canada a decade earlier. Low clouds hovered over a sprawling white plain, shaking out snow just as they had been doing non-stop for the past decade or so, and with every sign of continuing to do so.

The landscape—or snowscape—was littered with cones and blocks, scattered handfuls of them, half buried in graceful white mounds. They were the spires and roofs of the tallest buildings in what once had been Manhattan. Everything else was buried beneath 100 feet or more of snow. Most of the structures were skeletal, burned. All the world's great cities had been burned: New York, London, Paris, Berlin, Moscow, Beijing, and so many others. All torched by their terrified inhabitants, lashing out in an excess of terror, willing to set the world ablaze for a final brief flare-up of heat and light. Bereft of life, the New York scene was filled with a torrent of noise, a violent, never-ending clamor: the sound of mile-thick glaciers driving southward through the valleys.

The killing cold had not completely engulfed the southern hemisphere: Latin America, Africa, South Asia. These southlands held what remained of the human race. But global cooling had left their climates dry, arid, barren, with vast stretches of flat tundra and red sandy wastes, resembling nothing so much as the Gobi Desert. Within a few generations, the species will have reverted back to the Stone Age.

Planetary processes are flexible, not rigid. Not icebound for all time. Earth's orbital variations create cycles of advancing and retreating ice ages. It has happened many times before; it will happen again. The Deep Freeze will not last. There's a thaw due, in about 10,000 years—a mere eyeblink in cosmic time.

To many of us, ice ages are a phenomenon of the distant past, as likely to reappear as dinosaurs or Neanderthal man. Yet, the reality is that ice ages are a natural and reoccurring part of the earth's ever-restive climatic cycles, and a new epoch of sub-freezing temperatures could begin to cover as much as a third of the planet's land with immense glaciers within a matter of years.

William H. Calvin, a theoretical neurophysiologist at the University of Washington in Seattle, wrote an article for *The Atlantic Monthly* in 1998 titled "The Great Climate Flip-Flop." In his article, Calvin theorizes that greenhouse warming caused by the burning of fossil fuels could—paradoxically—lead to a sudden and drastic cooling of our climate severe enough to threaten the end of civilization. "One of the most shocking scientific realizations of all time has slowly been dawning on us," Calvin writes. "The earth's climate does great flip-flops every few thousand years, and with breathtaking speed. We could go back to ice-age temperatures within a decade—and judging from recent discoveries, an abrupt cooling could be triggered by our current global-warming trend."

As Calvin points out in his article, a sudden cooling of the earth's climate could come on so rapidly that we would not have time to make changes in our agricultural production—for instance, by genetically altering crops to grow in colder conditions. As a result, the world could face the worst food shortages in history, with potentially billions of people starving to death in a relatively short time.

Many other climatologists and glaciologists have also forecast a looming ice age. During the 1980s, ice cores taken from deep within glaciers in Greenland and Antarctica, as well as cores brought up from the sea floor of the North Atlantic and ancient lake beds, have convinced scientists that glaciers could surge outward from the polar regions in an astonishingly short time.

How quickly could our climate change? In the mid-1990s, glaciologist Kendrick Taylor of Nevada's Desert Research Institute studied a core from the Greenland Ice Sheet and found a temperature fluctuation in some places of 18 degrees Fahrenheit in as little as three years. To put this dramatic temperature change in perspective, a 2 degree drop in mean global temperatures during the thirteenth century brought on what is known as "The Little Ice Age," a period of intense cold that caused glaciers to grow throughout the northern and mountainous regions of Europe. The massive sheets of ice crushed entire villages and towns, and brought on widespread starvation and waves of mass migration.

A WORLD OF ICE

Prior to the nineteenth century, scientists had no clue that ice ages had once dominated the earth's climate. Early geologists had noted certain oddities in rock formations—such as huge granite boulders lying atop limestone far from the place where they had formed—but the prevailing belief then was that the boulders had been moved by the raging waters of the Biblical flood. Then, in the early 1800s, Swiss civil engineer Ignace Venetz began studying rock debris and sediment that had obviously been carried far from their original location. He also examined strange parallel grooves in the local surface bedrock that he realized had to have been carved out by some immensely powerful force. After years of geological research, Venetz concluded that both the debris fields and the grooves in the bedrock were the result of the same phenomenon: the steady advance and then retreat of massive glaciers during prehistoric times. In 1829, the Swiss scientist put forward convincing evidence that the ice had captured sediment and rocks in its frozen grasp as it moved inexorably across Switzerland. The combination of abrasive rocks and ice had not only cut grooves in the bedrock, but also carved out huge U-shaped depressions that later became either dry valleys or lake beds as the ice age ended and the glaciers melted away.

The new theory that an ice age had once covered an immense area of the world with glaciers a mile or more thick stunned the nineteenth-century scientific community. The revolutionary concept also brought fierce opposition from churchmen who insisted that the movement of rocks and sediment from one region to another was a direct result of Noah's flood described in the Bible. The objections of church leaders were soon silenced as evidence of not just one but many past ice ages began to pour in from scientists on every continent. Agassiz's theory fit hand in glove with the geological evidence that ancient ice ages had left in their wake. By the twentieth century, there was little doubt that advancing glaciers had ground out the immense cavities in mid-North America that later filled with meltwater and became the Great Lakes, the largest body of fresh water on Earth. Glaciers also formed Yosemite Valley; Lock Ness; innumerable valleys and lake beds on every continent; and fiords in Alaska, Antarctica, British Columbia, Chile, New Zealand, and Scotland. Scientists now understood that ice ages had not only radically and repeatedly changed the earth's climate—killing off entire plant and animal species in the process—but had also physically altered the topography of the planet in profound ways.

Today we know that the climate of the earth has cooled dramatically and repeatedly in prehistoric eras, with 10 ice ages descending upon the earth in the past one million years alone. The most recent ice age reached its peak 18,000 to 20,000 years ago. At that time, great ice sheets covered the land in North America, at one point reaching all the way south to the Ohio River valley, while in Europe glaciers buried the continent as far south as Switzerland. In the southern hemisphere, past ice ages have given birth to glaciers in Australia, South America, and Antarctica. Stretching away from the glaciers were vast areas of tundra where the ground was frozen solid and only sparse vegetation appeared during the short spring and summer months. It was a time when wooly mammoths roamed the earth, and only Neanderthal humans—with their special physical traits adapted to the extreme cold—could survive in Europe. Even parts of the tropics fell victim to the ice, with mountain glaciers forming in Hawaii, New Guinea, and Africa. Indeed, no place on earth escaped the terrible consequences of the massive ice sheets that ruled the weather of the world.

Scientists estimate that precipitation fell as much as 50 percent during the last ice age, bringing semi-arid or even desert conditions to once well-watered and vegetated areas. Heavy concentrations of dust particles taken from ice cores in Greenland and Antarctica point to a planet that was far more arid than it is today, and to the formation of vast sand dunes in Africa and Central America. The ice sheets captured so much of the earth's water that global sea level fell approximately 400 feet, exposing huge expanses of continental shelves that today lie submerged beneath the waves. As the newly exposed shelves dried out, their surfaces turned to dust, and the tiny particles of debris were carried all over the world by the winds, under the arid conditions that prevailed in the mid-latitudes between the ice sheets and the equator. There is also scientific evidence that the vast Amazon rainforest—a critical component of today's environment—fragmented into much smaller sections of jungle as precipitation plummeted and trees and plants died out.

The weight of the massive glaciers was so great that they actually depressed the earth's crust, in some areas as much as 2,600 feet! Today, many of these land masses—Scandinavia, for instance—now free of the incalculable weight of ice sheets miles thick, are slowly rising again.

Past ice ages also caused huge icebergs to calf off glaciers in both the Arctic and Antarctic regions and to drift out to sea. At times, these icebergs were so numerous that they covered half the world's oceans, and lowered the surface temperature of the sea by as much as 50 degrees Fahrenheit in the polar regions and perhaps 45 degrees in the tropical oceans. These glacial periods began at approximately 100,000-year intervals, lasted for an average of 90,000 years, and were then followed by 10,000-year interglacial eras—such as the one we now live in— during which the climate warmed. As the great ice sheets melted, the sea levels rose, warmer weather returned, and plant and animal species began to thrive in regions once covered with ice or reduced to barren tundra. The present interglacial period has also enabled diverse human civilizations to form all over the world, and made possible the progress of Homo sapiens from primitive hunter-gatherers to modern humans.

HOW COULD IT HAPPEN?

Given the profound effect that past ice ages have had on the earth's plant and animal species, including humans, the question arises: Could it happen again? Is it possible that in the decades or centuries ahead, titanic sheets of ice could spread out from the poles and once again cover the continents?

The answer is that it is not only possible, it is inevitable. Another ice age is coming, and there isn't a thing we can do to stop the advance of the glaciers. As surely as the sun rises and sets, sometime in the future, ice sheets a mile or more thick will again surge over the land, bulldozing skyscrapers and every other human structure in Chicago, New York, London, Stockholm, Moscow, Beijing, and thousands of other cities and towns in the higher latitudes of the Northern and southern hemispheres. Fertile farmlands will disappear beneath the ice or become useless frozen tundra, and the oceans will be covered with massive icebergs, making the shipping of food and trade goods impossible. As global temperatures plunge, scores of plant and animal species will freeze to death and vanish from the earth's ecosystem.

The origins of the next ice age lie both here on earth and in the far reaches of space. Scientists now understand much about the natural forces that bring on ice ages, but there is still wide disagreement about how these mechanisms work and interact. To identify the specific causes of ice ages, climatologists must solve a complicated scenario, for they not only have to find out why the earth has continuously gone through cycles of glacial and interglacial climate shifts, but also discover why our climate often suddenly warms for short periods during glacial periods and abruptly cools dramatically during interglacial times.

Perhaps the most widely accepted scientific explanation for the onset and end of major ice ages is the Milankovitch theory, which links the earth's climatic shifts to cyclical changes in the planet's circumnavigation of the sun. Named after Serbian astronomer Milutin Milankovitch, who conducted his research in the early 1900s, the theory argues that variations in the earth's orbit have a direct impact on the advance and retreat of ice ages. Milankovitch cites three main variations that directly affect climate conditions on earth. The first is eccentricity, which is simply the shape of the planet's orbit around the sun. The earth's orbit is not a circle but an ellipse, which oscillates from more elliptic to less elliptic over cycles of 100,000 years. The effect is that our planet is alternately farther from the sun or closer to the sun, meaning that the amount of solar radiation reaching the earth's surface can vary greatly from season to season. Scientists are now in general agreement that the larger the difference in seasonal climate conditions, the greater the chances are that an ice age will form.

The second source of variation in how much solar radiation reaches different parts of the earth involves what is known as "axial tilt," which refers to the inclination of the earth's axis in relation to the planet's plane of orbit around the sun. The earth wobbles on its axis and this wobble—up to 1.2 degrees on either side of the average tilt of 23.3 degrees—occurs over cycles of 41,000 years. Axial tilt affects the differences between summer and winter temperatures in both the northern and southern hemispheres. Less axial tilt results in a more equal distribution of the amount of solar radiation reaching the polar and equatorial regions. This causes warmer winters and cooler summers. When the atmosphere during the winter is warmer, the air can hold more moisture and produce more snow, which accumulates in glaciers surrounding the poles and in mountainous areas. During the cooler summers that follow, less snow melts, and year by year the ice sheets grow. Research conducted by the National Oceanographic and Atmospheric Agency's National Geophysical Data Center suggests that when northern-hemisphere summers are coolest and winters are warmest, ice sheets can form over vast areas of North America and Europe.

The third variable that Milankovitch notes is known as precession, which involves the timing of the earth's spring and fall equinoxes when the sun is positioned directly over the equator. Currently, the equinoxes fall on March 21 and December 21. However, due to gravitational influences of the moon and other planets, the timing of the equinoxes also varies. When the equinoxes coincide with the earth's closest and farthest approaches to the sun, greater seasonal contrasts take place. These heightened differences in summer and winter climate conditions can bring about a shift of as much as 25 percent in the amount of solar radiation reaching the higher latitudes, and directly contribute to the advance or retreat of ice sheets.

Major ice ages have occurred in the past when the eccentricity in the earth's orbit, axial tilt, and the precession of equinoxes have all coincided to bring the northern hemisphere the least amount of solar radiation. Although changes in the shape of the earth's orbit around the sun and variations in the planet's axis of rotation can trigger ice ages, several other factors may be involved in the abrupt and often severe climate changes that have occurred in past millennia.

The most probable of these natural mechanisms is a sudden change in the flow of the Gulf Stream, an ocean current often called the "river in the sea" that carries warm water from the Gulf of Mexico up the eastern seacoast of the United States. Off northern Canada, the Gulf Stream merges with the North Atlantic Current, which moves east through the Atlantic Ocean to Europe.

The Gulf Stream has the flow of a hundred Amazon Rivers, and the heat it transfers from the Gulf of Mexico across the Atlantic keeps northern Europe 9 to 18 degrees warmer in winter than the region would be if the warmth from the current did not bathe the continent. The Gulf Stream is part of a group of currents that could be compared to a continuous conveyor belt that loops around the Atlantic in a clockwise direction. The immense amount of water that the current carries from the Gulf of Mexico to the North Atlantic is not only warmer than the surrounding sea, it is also saltier. When the current reaches the seas between Greenland and Norway, winds blowing from the Arctic cool the surface water. This combination of colder ocean temperatures and high salinity makes the surface water denser and causes it to sink into the depths. As the dense water sinks, it acts like an engine pulling the warmer water behind it forward, ensuring the continuous flow of the Gulf Stream.

> If the Gulf Stream were suddenly to cease flowing, the nations of Europe would face catastrophic consequences as temperatures across the continent would plunge precipitously.

For millennia past, the North Atlantic current has given Europe a relatively temperate climate, and largely made possible agriculture and the development of civilization on the continent. The comparatively mild winters and warm summers that have prevailed in Europe for thousands of years are not the norm for land masses around the world at the same northerly latitudes. For instance, most of the populations of Canada and the United States live between the latitudes of 30 and 40 degrees north, yet the majority of the people in Europe live 10 to 15 degrees farther north. Paris is at almost 49 degrees latitude, putting the City of Light at the same latitude as southern Canada. London and Berlin, which lie at roughly 52 degrees, are both farther north than Newfoundland, while most of the major cities of Scandinavia are as close to the North Pole as parts of Alaska. If the Gulf Stream were suddenly to cease flowing, the nations of Europe would face catastrophic consequences as temperatures across the continent would plunge precipitously. The failure of the current would also impact the rest of the world because a colder Europe would chill regional climates as far south as the tropics.

Is it possible that the Gulf Stream could suddenly shut down? Yes! The Gulf Stream has ceased flowing several times in the past, and it is all but certain that the warm river in the sea will fail again at some time in the future. Several natural processes could bring about a disruption in the northeast flow of the Gulf Stream. Perhaps the most likely of these is an increase in the amount of fresh water flowing into the North Atlantic. Even a relatively small surge of fresh water could dilute the dense, salty Gulf Stream. If this happened, the less dense water would not sink into the depths of the North Atlantic, and the natural engine that pulls the current across the sea would suddenly shut down. Fresh water could flood into the North Atlantic from at least three possible sources. If an ice dam were to form across one of the hundreds of long, deep fiords of Greenland or Canada's large Baffin Island, the dam would bottle up a huge reservoir of fresh water when inland glaciers partially melt during the summer months. As has happened countless times in the past, the increasing volume of water trapped in the flooded fiord would eventually burst through the dam and surge out into the North Atlantic. If the pulse of fresh water were large enough, when it reached the Gulf Stream it could dilute the salt content of the current enough to shut down the flow.

Another possible scenario is that the warming of the planet brought on by the burning of fossil fuels might lessen the wind chill in the North Atlantic. When the winds get warmer, they lose some of their cooling power. Because these strong Arctic winds are essential to salt sinking, a drop in wind chill could slow or stop the flow of the Gulf Stream.

The third event that might cause the life-giving current to shut down is that global warming might cause a breakup of the immense Greenland Ice Sheet, sending a flotilla of icebergs into the North Atlantic. When the bergs inevitably begin to melt, the fresh water they release would dilute the dense salt water of the Gulf Stream in the same way as a flood from a fiord, and bring the current to a screeching halt.

Whatever the cause, if the Gulf Stream stopped carrying heat across the Atlantic to warm Europe, plant and animal species across the continent would be devastated. Agriculture and the raising of animals for meat would fail almost immediately, and the haunting prospect of mass starvation would fall over the continent like a cold, dark shadow. Undoubtedly, there would also be financial chaos as well as a quantitative leap in the need for fossil fuels to heat homes and power industries. Governments, faced with the impossible task of procuring enough food and fuel to sustain their nations, would inevitably fail. Were this to happen, political anarchy and civil unrest would sweep the continent.

History tells us that whenever there is a power vacuum in a country and widespread discontent among the people, the military steps in and assumes power. It has happened countless times in the past, and there is every reason to believe that it would happen in Europe if a sudden subarctic climate shift threw the continent into chaos. If the nations of Europe were suddenly faced with the prospect of their vast populations starving or freezing to death, what possible solution would they have but to invade food- and fuel-producing areas in more southerly latitudes?

If such invasions were to occur, the undeveloped countries of Africa, the Middle East, South America, and Asia could not possibly defend themselves against the militarily superior forces of the European nations with their planes, missiles, modern armaments, and well-trained troops. A new wave of colonialism could wash across the globe with the French reasserting sovereignty over North Africa, the Belgians taking back the Congo, the British marching into the oil-producing Arab Emirates on the Persian Gulf, the Italians seizing Ethiopia, the Germans conquering Argentina, and the Russians invading Turkey.

Is such a scenario far-fetched? Is it inconceivable that the democratic and peaceful nations of Europe might invade the undeveloped countries to the south? The answer is that there might well be no alternative.

In his *Atlantic Monthly* article, "The Great Climate Flip-Flop," William Calvin writes that, "Plummeting crop yields will cause some powerful countries to try to take over their neighbors or distant lands— if only because their armies, unpaid and lacking food, will go marauding, both at home and across the borders. The better-organized countries will attempt to use their armies, before they fall apart entirely, to take over countries with significant remaining resources, driving out or starving their inhabitants if not using modern weapons to accomplish the same end: eliminating competitors for the remaining food.

"Europe's vulnerability is particularly easy to analyze. Present-day Europe has 650 million people. It has excellent soils, and largely grows its own food. It could no longer do so if it lost the extra warming from the North Atlantic current. If Europe had weather like Canada's, which is at the same latitude, it could feed only 1 out of 23 present-day Europeans."

If you were the prime minister of Britain, the president of France, or the chancellor of Germany, and you had to choose between watching millions of your citizens starve or freeze to death and seizing control of foreign territories, which would you choose? The European powers could even make the argument that such invasions were morally justified. After all, most of the people of Africa are poverty-stricken and suffering under corrupt dictatorships. At the same time, millions of square miles of land that could be used for agriculture are presently uncultivated.

If the nations of Europe were to seize power in large areas of Africa, they would undoubtedly modernize local industry and agriculture, provide widespread medical care, boot out the dictators, and bring peace and prosperity to tens of millions of Africans. The seizure of the smaller Persian Gulf oil-producing states such as Oman, the United Arab Emirates, Qatar, Bahrain, and Kuwait could also be morally defended. After all, most of these states are ruled by feudal sultans who have bled Europe for years with exorbitant oil prices. Few countries on earth would shed a tear if one or more European powers were to march into the region and seize control of oil production. An invasion of Central or South America would be harder to justify, but would probably occur nevertheless. Indeed, if the sudden failure of the Gulf Stream were to trigger another ice age, not only in Europe but throughout the northern hemisphere, the United States, Canada, China, and Japan might also have to consider invading food- and fuel-producing lands to the south.

Although both a sudden change in the flow of the Gulf Stream and a change in the pattern of solar radiation reaching the earth can start ice ages, several other natural forces can bring on massive glaciation. As mentioned previously in this book, an asteroid or meteor impact with earth could eject enough dust and debris into the atmosphere to block out sunlight and cause surface temperatures to plunge, starting another ice age. Volcanic eruptions that spewed large quantities of ash and debris into the air could have the same effect, albeit the eruptions would have to be both massive and sustained to eject enough material to change our climate on a worldwide scale.

A newly proposed theory suggests that dust and tiny meteors from space could also impact our climate in dramatic ways. In an article in *Science* magazine, researchers Richard A. Muller of the Lawrence Berkeley National Laboratory and Gordon J. MacDonald of the International Institute for Applied Systems Analysis reported that cyclical changes in the location of the earth's orbit directly affect the amount of extraterrestrial debris entering the earth's atmosphere. Just as in the event of an asteroid strike or a huge volcanic eruption, the more dust and debris in the earth's atmosphere, the less sunlight we would receive, and the colder our climate would become.

MacDonald and Muller note that as the earth's orbital plane slowly tilts in and out of alignment with the sun's plane of rotation, in cycles of 100,000-plus years, the planet encounters varying amounts of space debris, and the differences in the quantity of extraterrestrial material entering our atmosphere directly affects our climate. "As far as we know," Muller said, "none of the present climate models include the effects of dust and meteors. And yet, our data suggests that such accretion played a dominant role in the climate for the last million years. If we wish to make accurate predictions, we must understand the role played by such material."

Although the scientific community has differing theories for what causes major and minor ice ages, there is no doubt that massive glaciation has occurred repeatedly in the past and will strike again in the future, perhaps within our lifetimes. An article in the *Encarta Encyclopedia* says, "Evidence from both land and sea environments indicates that, at least prior to the human-induced global warming of the last two centuries, the worldwide climate has been cooling naturally for several thousand years."

Another ice age may have already begun. If you live in North America, Europe, Siberia, China, Japan, or any of the regions of the higher southern latitudes, your fate may not lie in your hands but in the whimsy of natural forces that humans can barely fathom, much less change. Your home, your workplace, the power plants that warm you, and the grain fields that feed you, all these could disappear beneath titanic ice sheets within a short span of years. With all of our scientific and technological milestones, the human race is still but a pawn in the chess game played out by terrestrial and extraterrestrial forces that will forever be beyond our control.

> Massive glaciation has occurred repeatedly in the past and will strike again in the future, perhaps within our lifetimes.

MEGA-TSUNAMIS

In Charleston, South Carolina, on an April weekday at about 4 P.M., an observer looking seaward would have seen what looked like several dozen surfboards sliding down the face of an onrushing green wave. Surfboards, but no riders. A lively port city, Charleston Harbor bustles with commercial ships and barges. But ordinarily, there's no surfing.

The oncoming wave rushed in. What looked like surfboards resolved themselves into toy boats—several handfuls of toy boats, scattered on the sea and now sliding down the face of the wave.

Accompanying the wave was a wall of noise. This was not the rhythmic rise and fall of the surf, but rather a grinding, rumbling roar, as much felt as seen, shaking Charleston with mounting vibrations.

The wave closed in on the waterfront's piers and wharves, cranes and warehouses. Observers now saw what seemed unbelievable: The toy boats were actually real boats and ships—fishing boats, garbage barges, freighters, container ships, oil tankers, naval and Coast Guard vessels, all dwarfed on the surface of the giant, surging wave.

These observers would witness Charleston's last moments. Some of them had given up any fight to survive and resigned themselves to the inevitable. Others had remained behind, either out of disbelief, or perversity, or sheer pigheaded obstinacy. And some had fallen behind in the mad exodus inland, wounded and despairing, and saw the aquatic destruction in all its fearful pageantry.

But most of Charleston's former residents were facing the other way, fleeing the doomed city, leaving it to the rising wall of water. Many of the city's boulevards, squares, and sidewalks were empty. The exodus was on. However, the alert had been tardy, with a short lead time, and a city cannot empty in an instant. A limited number of freeways led landward, too few to adequately handle the overload of vehicles trying to flee.

It was unimaginable, unthinkable. It had never happened before, at least not in recorded history. But recorded history is but a few clock-ticks in geologic time—or, in this case, subaquatic time. Planet Earth is four fifths water, and scientists know more about the surface of the moon than about the bottom of the sea, where there lies a complex undersea domain of submerged mountains and deep-plunging marine trenches.

CHAPTER 6: MEGA-TSUNAMIS

In the Atlantic, the major undersea mountain ranges run north-south. In the mid-North Atlantic latitudes, a hulking seamount's western slope was undermined by a crack in the earth's crust, a vent connected to the seething red-hot molten magma underlying the tectonic plates. The vent allowed the passage not of magma, but of volcanic gases, bottled up under ever-increasing pressure from below. The gas had leaked through crevices in the rock, permeating it, weakening it. Over millennia, much of the seamount's western base had become hollowed out from within.

Fewer than 12 hours before the wave loomed off Charleston, the seamount had reached the breaking point. The western slope collapsed and cubic miles of rock and silt crumbled from its flanks, falling into an undersea trench yawning beside it. Propelling the massive underwater avalanche was the buildup of volcanic gases, now freed, accelerating the slide of the massive amounts of debris, and pouring extra energy into an event already possessing megatons of potential energy—energy that had to go somewhere. Huge pressure waves expanded out from the epicenter of the crash.

The Atlantic stirred, heaving in the heart of its depths. The ocean's surface began to rise, expanding outward, rushing shoreward in all directions. The greatest seaquake of all time had generated turbulence to match. The result was a tsunami, the correct term for what's commonly known as a tidal wave. But this was no mere tsunami, it was a mega-tsunami, the biggest in history. A mega-tsunami of such force that human history would henceforth be measured in two periods: that which came before the big wave struck, and that which came after.

The circular wave raced shoreward, speeding toward the Atlantic coasts of the Americas, Africa, Europe, Iceland, and Greenland. Onward rushed the wall of water, a gentle giant lifting ships in its path.

Orbiting satellites detected the event. Operators monitoring computer screens literally reeled in shock from what the sensors were reporting. They could hardly believe what they were seeing. But the sensors told the truth, and the numbers filled in the details: Atlantic coastal areas were about to be struck by a mega-tsunami. At its worst, along the North American coastline, the wave would be 300 feet high. At its weakest, the wave would still be more than 150 feet high.

DOOMSDAY

Several hours elapsed while the scientists calculated the data's frightening conclusions and passed the information along to their various governments. It would be about eight hours between the issuing of the first official warnings to the public and the moment when the wave would reach shore.

Eight hours. Scant time for the greatest mass migration in recorded history; time only, really, to create a catastrophic panic. In Europe, Africa, and the Americas, scores of millions of people lay in the path of destruction. All the flights of all the refugees fleeing the great catastrophes of human history combined could hardly have matched the inland rush to escape the mega-tsunami.

On the East Coast of the United States, the distance needed to out-race the wave was a minimum of six miles. Eight would be preferable. Of course, no highway system in the world, not even that of the car-loving United States, was equipped to handle the volume now thronging the inland thoroughfares. Progress was at a crawl when not stopped entirely. Fear multiplied the number of accidents and collisions. When a car broke down and blocked a lane, the other cars would bull it over to the roadside, shoving it out of the way. Where escape lay across solid ground, when forward movement halted, people could and did abandon their cars, streaming across the landscape in zig-zagging lines that from overhead looked like lines of ants.

For Charleston, as for so many others, the end was nigh. The moment of impact had arrived. The mega-tsunami came on, ushered in by a torrent of noise, a roaring as of a thousand Niagaras. A mountain of water, climbing higher and higher, blotted out the eastern sky. The wave was emerald green, streaked and marbled, glass slick. All fell before its inexorable advance.

The city was obliterated, like a wasp's nest washed away by a fire hose. What remained looked like a sprinkling of stumps rising from a bed of mud. The stumps were city blocks that had been left standing. Charleston was no more. Its fate was shared by every city, village, and settlement within roughly six miles of the Atlantic coast, from Maine to Mexico.

The wave raced inland without even a pause.

———————————————■———————————————

In the Canary archipelago off the northwest coast of Africa, a time bomb ticks away in the bowels of a volcano called Cumbre Vieja on the island of La Palma. When the bomb goes off, countless millions of people will die on both sides of the Atlantic Ocean.

The British Broadcasting Company (BBC) News recently reported that research by geologists has turned up chilling evidence that the western flank of the volcano is unstable and could collapse into the sea, spawning a 3,000-foot-high dome of water. The resulting mega-tsunami—or huge tidal wave—would be higher than any in recorded history, and would travel outward across the Atlantic at 500 miles per hour. A tsunami of this incredible magnitude would devastate the coasts of Africa, Europe, North America, and South America.

Dr. Steven Ward of the University of California and Dr. Simon Day of the Benfield Greig Hazard Research Center at University College, London, write in *Geophysical Research Letters* that a buildup of groundwater could destabilize a block of lava more than 300 cubic miles in size. They estimate that this immense mass of rock would rush into the sea at 330 feet per second. The energy released by the collapse would equal the entire U.S. electricity consumption for six months and create a dome of water 2,950 feet high. The resulting tsunami—larger than any in recorded history—would travel outward from the Canary Islands at 500 miles per hour.

Dr. Day told the BBC's *Science Horizon* program that, "This event would be so huge that it would affect not only the people on the island, but also people way over on the other side of the Atlantic Ocean—people who've never heard of La Palma."

A WALL OF WATER

Affect might be too tame a word. Scientists calculate that if the Cumbre Vieja volcano collapses into the sea, the titanic avalanche of rock will generate tsunami waves more than 300 feet high when they reach the coasts of Portugal, Spain, and west Africa. Such immense waves would totally obliterate all animal and plant life—including humans—along vast stretches of coastline, and then flood far inland, drowning everyone and everything in their path. Although dissipated by distance, the main tsunami surge will likely still be more than 40 feet high when it strikes England, Ireland, and France. Port cities like Portsmouth, Cork, and Cherbourg will be laid to waste as the great wave sweeps away docks, railyards, roads, buildings, and homes.

As great as the devastation will be in Europe, the loss of life and property will pale in comparison to the cataclysm that the towering tsunami would inflict upon the Americas. Nine hours after the collapse of the Cumbre Vieja volcano, the shores of South America as far south as Brazil will be inundated under 130-foot waves, while to the north, the fiord-pierced Atlantic coast of Greenland will disappear beneath the relentless advance of the mega-tsunami.

Yet it is the islands and countries of the Caribbean and the Atlantic shoreline of the United States that would suffer the hammer blow of the gargantuan tsunami sweeping in from the east. From Port of Spain north to Canada, a monstrous wave 160 feet high will assault the land.

In the Caribbean, the tsunami will entirely wash over low-lying islands and atolls, sweeping away everything in its path and leaving lifeless hulks of coral, stone, and sand behind. Poor communications in the area will mean that millions do not receive the tsunami warning in time. When the great wave hits, fishermen will be casting their nets offshore, people will be doing laundry in homes a few feet above sea level, and children will be playing in the gentle surf of placid lagoons from Martinique to the coast of Mexico. All will perish, their bodies swept out to sea to become food for the fishes.

In the United States, the death toll will be far more catastrophic because the highest population of people is living in vulnerable areas along the shore. Miami, Charleston, Norfolk, New York, Boston, and hundreds of other coastal cities and towns, with tens of millions of residents, will bear the full assault of the mega-tsunami.

> Imagine eight million people all trying to flee New York City at once.

Because the giant wave will take nine hours to cross the Atlantic from the Canary Islands to the U.S. eastern seaboard, modern communications systems will quickly spread the warning. Private and public transportation will carry tens of millions inland to safety on higher ground. But not all will make it. Hundreds of thousands will jam airports, railway stations, and bus terminals, only to discover that all planes, trains, and buses are already full. Imagine eight million people all trying to flee New York City at once, with millions more stampeding out of low-lying areas of Long Island and New Jersey. And what of those on the margins of society, the homeless, the hospitalized, the mentally impaired, the tens of thousands lying helpless in nursing homes? Will the strong stop to help them, or will it be survival of the fittest? One may only hope that if a mega-tsunami does someday race across the Atlantic toward the eastern coasts of the Americas, people will display the same altruism that New Yorkers and Washingtonians showed the victims of the September 11 tragedy.

Because much of the Atlantic coastal plain of the United States consists of estuaries, bays, river mouths, and low-lying land, the tsunami would race inland as far as six miles, destroying everything before it, leaving behind a battlefield-like landscape of shattered human structures and flattened trees.

As terrifying as this specter is, the actual event could be even worse. In the BBC News article, Dr. Day cautions that if the speed of the landslide proved to be 490 feet per second, not the 330 feet per second assumed, that could double the height of the tsunami. Assuming that Dr. Day's more pessimistic prognosis is correct, the Caribbean and the Atlantic coast of North American would vanish beneath a tsunami more than 300 feet high! One can only shudder at the thought of how far inland such a monstrous wave would reach.

How real is the threat? Scientists studying the geology of the La Palma volcano take the danger very seriously. "If I were living in Miami or New York and heard that the Cumbre Vieja was erupting, I would keep a very close eye on the news," says vulcanologist Bill McGuire, director of the Benfield Greig Hazard Research Center.

The Geological Society of London is also concerned that a collapse of the Cumbre Vieja volcano could put lives and property in peril all along the Atlantic coast of England. The Society recently wrote to the United Kingdom Science Minister, Lord Salisbury, to make him aware of the dangers posed by the looming mega-tsunami in the Atlantic. The

Society expressed the hope that he would take the issue as seriously as he has the threat from asteroid strikes.

How imminent is the danger that the western flank of the Cumbre Vieja volcano will break off and rush into the sea, spawning a mega-tsunami? Dr. Day told BBC News Online, "We think that we have to see some evidence of subterranean movement before there's a risk of collapse. The fact that we aren't seeing any movement gives us a lot of confidence Cumbre Vieja won't collapse spontaneously."

Great news, right? Now you can buy that beachfront condo on the Jersey shore and not have to worry about a tsunami sending you fleeing in terror for higher ground and turning your vacation home into kindling behind you. Well, before you rush off to the real estate office, perhaps you should read the "but" that Dr. Day adds to his prognosis. Having established that an eruption would be the most likely trigger of a collapse of the volcano, Dr. Day says, "But we've found that eruptions do tend to come in clusters. *And there've been two in the recent past.*" (Italics added.)

If you live within 25 miles of the Atlantic coast, the burning question is, which way do you bet?

DANGER FROM BENEATH

Although the collapse of the Cumbre Vieja volcano would probably spawn the deadliest Atlantic tsunami, a potential submarine landslide off the mid-Atlantic coast of the United States also poses the threat of inundating our shores beneath a wall of water. *Daily University Science News* recently reported that, "Potential landslides on the outer continental shelf and slope and the Mid-Atlantic coast could trigger tidal waves that might have devastating effects on populated coastal areas."

In a paper published in *Geology* magazine, Neal Driscoll of the Woods Hole Oceanographic Institution, and colleagues Jeffrey Weissel of Columbia University's Lamont-Doherty Earth Observatory and John Goff of the University of Texas at Austin, reported that newly discovered cracks along the edge of the continental shelf could be an early warning sign that the seafloor is unstable in these areas. The scientists have concluded that the cracks are actually holes caused by gas erupting through the seafloor. "We don't know the source of the gas, but it is clear that gas has played an important role in the formation of these features," Driscoll says. "The gas is trapped under layers of sediment on the shelf edge until some circumstance causes it to escape, blowing holes in the seafloor to form these large pockmark features we thought were cracks."

If a gas blowout should occur, the violent disruption of the seafloor could conceivably set off a submarine landslide, which would, in turn, cause a tsunami to form in the water above.

The implications of the submarine cracks spurred the interest of the National Science Foundation, and the research vessel Cape Hatteras was sent out to investigate the newly discovered phenomenon. The scientists used a special towed sonar array to image the seafloor, and found fissures as large as 4,900 feet across, 165 feet deep, and more than 3 miles long. Driscoll and Weissel admitted to being "a bit taken aback" by the apparent extent of the gas venting.

An article in the *Uniscience News*, a publication covering research at American universities, reports, "These cracks, together with evidence of past landslides in the same area, indicate the seafloor could slump, or slide downhill, like an avalanche, triggering the waves. Wave heights similar to the storm surge from a category-3 or -4 hurricane ... could occur along the Virginia-North Carolina coastline and lower Chesapeake Bay, the areas of highest risk."

The day after the report was aired, the media mobbed Driscoll, Goff, and Weissel, seeking further details about the possible cataclysm looming off the east coast of the United States. "We underestimated the excitement the paper would cause," Weissel said. Why would word that a giant wave might obliterate every coastal community between North Carolina and New Jersey cause any excitement?

The *Uniscience* article also points out a chilling historical parallel. "A 1929 tsunami from a landslide associated with a magnitude 7.2 earthquake on the Grand Banks [a submarine plateau off the east coast of Canada] left 51 dead along the [sparsely populated] south coast of Newfoundland. Tsunami wave heights recorded from that earthquake and landslide reached an estimated 40 feet in some areas along the coast."

If a 40-foot-high tsunami—as high as a four-story building—smashed into the heavily populated Mid-Atlantic coast of the United States, every home and commercial building within about a mile of shore would be swept away, along with any people inside.

When a fierce hurricane roars in from the tropical Atlantic, meteorologists can now model the probable course of the storm on computers and warn people living along endangered stretches of coast to get out before the hurricane hits. This will not be the case if a sudden submarine landslide on the continental shelf—which is just off our eastern seaboard—spawns a fast-moving tsunami. People will have very little time to flee beachfront homes and low-lying areas inland, and many will simply not make it.

"If a massive landslide occurred this close to the coast, you would only have about twenty minutes' warning," Weissel cautions. "With a hurricane, you often have hours or days. In that respect, the tsunami threat is even more acute."

The worst scenario would be if the tsunami struck on a hot summer afternoon when hundreds of thousands of vacationers are enjoying the sun and surf, from Long Island to Florida. Because tsunamis raise the sea level only slightly as they travel across deep water, it will be all but impossible for ships offshore—or planes flying overhead—to detect the killer wave as it races toward shore. Super-sensitive sensors aboard earth-monitoring satellites orbiting over the East Coast would undoubtedly detect the submarine landslide and the tsunami that followed. But the need to interpret the data and get a warning out to the media would eat up precious minutes. Even when the alert sounded, few on the beaches would have radios to hear it. Those who did would undoubtedly spread the alarm by panicking, so that an orderly evacuation would be highly unlikely; most would be lucky to make it to their vacation homes or cars before the wall of water hit.

In an eye-opening article in *Scientific American* in October 2000 titled, "Killer Waves on the East Coast?" science writer Sarah Simpson cautioned that, "With a sudden crumbling of the seafloor, the Atlantic Ocean would rise up and flatten Virginia Beach and Cape Hatteras. Giant waves might even surge up the Potomac River and *flood the U.S. capital.*" (Italics added.)

Imagine for a moment the chaos that would ensue if a towering tsunami suddenly inundated Washington, D.C. Should the president be in the White House, the First Family would have to flee to the upper floors or the attic. If the president happened to be in a motorcade on the way to some function, the Secret Service would have only fleeting moments to get him or her to the safety of some nearby rooftop. Senators, members of the House of Representatives, and their staffs would stampede down the marble halls for the elevators. The scene would be the same at the Justice Department, the Pentagon, and dozens of other government offices. The tsunami would destroy irreplaceable records and papers. The War Room of the White House—several floors underground—would flood to the ceiling.

The raging waters would short out communications and electronic security systems, causing a total breakdown of command and control. Intelligence-gathering computers, satellite uplinks, and secure telephone and Internet communications to foreign governments and U.S. embassies around the world would be knocked out. The president would have to rely heavily on slow-moving means to issue orders and gather information. This is, of course, assuming that the tsunami were 50 feet or less in height. If it were instead one of the monster waves that have swept over the coasts of the earth's islands and continents in years past, we won't have to worry about the president or the Congress communicating with the rest of the world. They'll all be dead. A leadership vacuum, widespread confusion, and panic would inevitably follow.

As frightening as is the prospect of an Atlantic Ocean tsunami devastating the east coast of the United States, the threat is far greater that monster waves will wreak havoc along the shores of the Pacific. The reason is that the Pacific basin is circled by the infamous "Ring of Fire," a series of submarine volcanic arcs and oceanic trenches that roughly follow the edges of the Pacific Plate. (For an explanation of plate tectonics, see Chapter 3.)

Geological activity along the Ring of Fire produces continuous volcanic eruptions, earthquakes, and submarine landslides, all of which shift massive amounts of water and produce tsunamis that radiate outward at great speed. A previously unknown seafloor landslide threat was recently discovered perilously close to the west coast. A news release put out by the American Geophysical Union reports that geologists at the Monterey Bay Aquarium Research Institute (MBARI) have uncovered startling new evidence of massive submarine landslides off the shore of Santa Barbara, California.

Although plate boundaries along the west coast of the United States often generate life-threatening geologic events, other sections of the Ring of Fire are even more active. In the southwest Pacific, the Indo-Australian plate dives under the Eurasian plate, producing frequent earthquakes, volcanic eruptions, and submarine landslides. Over the millennia, these violent upheavals of the earth have generated countless tsunamis that have devastated the coasts of the nearby island-nation of Indonesia.

Perhaps the best known of these tsunamis was the immense wave that was generated by the eruption of the volcanic island of Krakatau in 1883. Krakatau was one of the most powerful volcanic explosions in modern history. The eruption was so strong that the island literally blew apart with a sound that was heard nearly 3,000 miles away. The explosion spawned a train of towering tsunamis that swept over the nearby coasts of Java and Sumatra at an estimated height of more than 130 feet. One hundred sixty-three villages were destroyed, and 31,417 men, women, and children drowned.

Whatever the origin of a tsunami, when the huge wave strikes land— be it nearby islands or the coasts of continents thousands of miles away— death and destruction inevitably follow. In the past century, tsunamis have killed more than 50,000 people around the Pacific and destroyed billions of dollars worth of property.

One of the most lethal submarine landslide-generated tsunamis in recent years struck the northern coast of Papua New Guinea in 1988. Fifteen thousand people lived in the path of the huge wave, most of them in the small villages of Sissano, Nalol, Warapu, and Arop. Just before sunset, the ground began to shake and the villagers heard an ear-splitting boom. Yawning fissures opened on the beach, drawing a crowd of curious onlookers. Suddenly the water began to withdraw from the shore, as if pulled away by some mysterious force.

Moments later the villagers heard a roar like the sound of a jet plane coming from somewhere out to sea. The roar built steadily, riveting the people where they stood. Then they saw the immense wave coming, and men, women, and children turned as one and fled screaming from the beach. The tsunami broke offshore and surged inland, engulfing panicked people and destroying their fragile homes. Then a second towering wave swept in, followed shortly by a third. When the sea finally retreated, the four villages lay in ruins and 2,000 people were dead.

A dramatic account of the nightmarish events that can accompany a tsunami comes from P. Saint-Amand, a resident of Chile who witnessed a huge wave coming ashore in 1960. Saint-Amand writes, "The wave rushed over the land, covering and carrying away the houses, killing the animals that could not be evacuated, and carrying off some of the people who … had not left their homes. The waves continued all afternoon …. A group of mapuchis or Araucanian Indians even sacrificed a seven-year-old boy to the gods of the sea to try to calm the remorseless surf."

The fact that people living in a civilized country in the midst of the twentieth century could be so traumatized by a tsunami that they would revert to the primitive practice of human sacrifice to save themselves is powerful testimony to the horror and feeling of helplessness that these giant waves invoke in mankind.

In recent years, tsunamis have devastated the coasts of literally every country bordering the Pacific. Immense waves—often more than 100 feet high—have killed tens of thousands in Indonesia, Japan, Siberia, Alaska, North America, Central America, and South America. Yet, paradoxically, the largest tsunamis of all have not occurred around the Ring of Fire but in the Hawaiian Islands in the middle of the Pacific Ocean, thousands of miles from the nearest plate boundary. The islands are the tips of marine volcanoes—some extinct and some still active—which have risen thousands of feet from the ocean floor. The basaltic lava that built up the volcanoes came from a hot spot, a plume of molten magma that rose from the earth's fiery interior and burned its way through the crust, like a blowtorch through a sheet of plywood.

Many hot spots exist around the world—including one beneath Yellowstone Park—and wherever they are found, volcanism and earthquakes also occur. In Hawaii, the volcanic islands rise so steeply from the sea, and the slopes are often so latticed with fractures, that even a moderate earthquake can set off a huge landslide. Water seeping down into the fissures can also cause mountainsides to fail and plunge into the ocean.

A prehistoric slide on the island of Oahu created perhaps the largest submarine debris field yet discovered. Called the Nuuanu landslide, the fragments of mountainside that plunged into the ocean cover an astounding 8,900 square miles of seafloor. Jonathan Knight, in an article in *New Scientist* magazine, gives this vivid account of what the titanic event might have been like:

"Slabs of rock bigger than football fields tumbled into the water by the thousands. Hundreds of blocks the size of small towns followed. One—the size of New York City—finally came to rest 100 kilometers [62 miles] from shore. When the dust settled, a tenth of the island was gone."

The landslide caused a giant tsunami that raced outward in all directions. When the giant wave hit the nearby island of Molokai, it was at least 1,000 feet high. After inundating the shores of the Hawaiian islands, the tsunami sped east, west, north, and south across the vast expanse of the Pacific. From the Americas to Japan, the implacable wall of water struck coastlines with unimaginable fury. Millions of trees—including huge 1,000-year-old California Redwoods—were ripped up by their roots and sucked out to sea. Boulders the size of buildings were lifted up like feathers in the wind and carried far inland, and any animal unlucky enough to be near the ocean that day drowned in a maelstrom of swirling seawater. When the train of towering waves finally retreated, beaches had vanished, cliffs had collapsed, and huge swaths of shoreline around the perimeter of the Pacific had been swept clean of all vegetation and soil. No coast looked the same; every bay or river mouth was clogged with silt and debris, and no wild-animal habitat near the sea remained unscathed. The immense tsunami had changed the very face of the earth.

Scientists were not fully aware of the landslide danger in Hawaii until recent research by the U.S. Geological Survey (USGS) turned up evidence that entire mountainsides had slid into the sea in the not-too-distant past, spawning towering tsunamis. The startling research was largely the work of James Moore, a pioneering geologist with the USGS in Menlo Park, California. As early as 1964, Moore had noted large submarine debris fields off the coast of the Hawaiian island of Oahu, and proposed that the rock deposits had calved off the island and slid out onto the seafloor during large earthquakes. Most other geologists believed that the piles of debris were merely smaller marine volcanoes.

Faced with the skepticism of his colleagues, Moore put his theory aside until the 1980 eruption of Mount St. Helens. When the volcano blew apart, the entire north flank of the mountain slid into the valley below, proving that the slopes of volcanoes are highly susceptible to sudden landslides. "The whole idea that volcanoes fall apart raced through the [scientific] community after Mount St. Helens," says David Clague, a vulcanologist with the Monterey Bay Aquatic Research Institute in California. "Jim Moore was twenty years ahead of the curve."

Moore knew that suddenly dropping a chunk of rock the size of New York City into the ocean would spawn an immense wave, but he didn't realize just how big the tsunami would be until he began doing geologic research on the island of Lanai. While exploring the south side of the island, he came across fields of coral and seashells as high as 400 feet above the nearest beach. Only a tsunami five times as tall as the largest wave ever recorded on Hawaii could carry coral debris that far above sea level.

Yet, the evidence is that even larger waves have swept over the shores of the Hawaiian Islands in the past. In the 1940s, geologist Harold Stearns had also discovered coral debris high up on the volcanic slopes of Lanai. Incredibly, the deposits Stearns found *were more than 1,200 feet above sea level—three times higher than the coral Moore had uncovered!* To carry marine debris almost a quarter-mile above the surface of the Pacific would have taken a wave big enough to surge over the Golden Gate Bridge.

Could another huge landslide strike the Hawaiian Islands today, sending a gargantuan tsunami racing across the Pacific toward the Americas and Asia? The answer is that it not only could happen, but that it undoubtedly will. Satellite measurements show that the entire southern slope of the Kilauea volcano on Hawaii's Big Island is a titanic landslide waiting to happen. From the 4,000-foot-high peak of the volcano to its submarine terminus 24 miles offshore, Kilauea's south flank is creeping seaward at a rate of several inches a year, *making it the fastest-moving piece of land of its size on the planet Earth!* (Italics added.)

The section of Kilauea that's shifting seaward is much larger than the mountainside that slid into the ocean causing the skyscraper-high Lanai tsunami. Scientists speculate that if Kilauea collapses into the sea, it would create a seafloor debris field roughly the size of the immense Nuuanu landslide.

"On Kilauea we have the potential for a future landslide on the scale of Nuuanu," says Julia Morgan, a geologist at the University of Hawaii who has been monitoring Kilauea closely. Geologists presently have no way of predicting how large the falling pieces of slope will be. One thing is certain, however: If Kilauea calves off a block of basaltic lava as large as the New York City–size chunk of rock that plunged into the sea during the Nuuanu slide, a tsunami more than 1,000 feet high will inundate the Big Island of Hawaii, and hours later the largest waves ever witnessed by humanity will roll over the far-flung shores of the Pacific.

Although large coastal cities like Seattle, San Francisco, Los Angeles, Lima, Sydney, Hong Kong, Shanghai, and Tokyo will have several hours warning before the tsunami strikes, the logistics of evacuating tens of millions of people to higher ground will be insurmountable. In San Francisco, the bridges will be bumper to bumper; in Los Angeles, gridlock will bring cars on the freeways to a screeching halt; in Hong Kong, panic will set in as millions stampede through narrow streets in a desperate attempt to reach the safety of the hills. Trapped in gargantuan traffic jams and floods of fleeing pedestrians, tens of millions of men, women, and children will simply not be able to escape the low-lying shore areas before the train of monster waves arrives. Few of those trapped near the ocean will survive, and those that do will have little to return to. The tsunami will reduce homes, factories, and office buildings to rubble; twist apart steel bridges; undermine highways and railroads; wash away airport runways; and leave behind a stinking layer of sand and silt peppered with decomposing human bodies.

Yet, as terrible as will be the toll taken by a tsunami spawned by the collapse of a volcano into the sea, the death and destruction will pale in comparison to the carnage that would follow the arrival of the great "mother of tsunamis"—an asteroid impact with one of the earth's oceans. Los Alamos National Laboratory staff member Jack G. Hills points out that when an asteroid impacts solid ground, it dissipates its energy quickly and in a comparatively small volume. However, if that same asteroid were to come down in the ocean, it would generate waves that retained enormous amounts of energy as they radiated out across the surrounding sea.

> Another mega-tsunami is on the way, and there will be nothing humans can do to stop it.

These waves can scour thousands of kilometers of coastline with debris and towering walls of water. A June 2002 news release from the Los Alamos National Laboratory in Albuquerque, New Mexico, reported that scientists using new super-fast computers had modeled an asteroid impact with one of the earth's oceans and come to some truly hair-raising conclusions. "Computer scientists Galen Gisler and Bob Weaver from the Los Alamos Thermonuclear Applications Group and Michael Gittings of Science Applications International Corp. created simulations of six different asteroid scenarios, varying the size and composition of a space visitor hitting a three-mile-deep patch of ocean at a speed of 45,000 miles an hour.

"The Big Kahuna in their model was an iron asteroid one kilometer [.62 mile] in diameter; they also looked at half-sized, or 500-meter [1,640-feet], and quarter-sized variants, and at asteroids made of stone, roughly 40 percent less dense than iron. 'We found that the one-kilometer iron asteroid struck with an impact equal to about 1.5 trillion tons of TNT, and produced a jet of water *more than 12 miles high*,' Giesler said." (Italics added.)

The story adds, "The model predicts that wave velocities for the largest [one kilometer] asteroid will be roughly 380 miles an hour … [and] … the initial tsunami waves are more than half a mile high, abating to about two-thirds of that height 40 miles in all directions from the point of impact."

If an asteroid impact generated a tsunami of this immense size in the ocean off a heavily populated shoreline, millions would be drowned within minutes.

What are the chances of an asteroid one kilometer in diameter hurtling into one of the earth's oceans, which cover two thirds of the planet's surface? The Australian Spaceguard Survey has estimated the impact risks posed by different-size asteroids, projecting that asteroids approximately one kilometer in diameter strike the earth at an average interval of once every 100,000 years. The problem is, this is an *average interval*. A one-kilometer asteroid could collide with the earth tomorrow or a million years from now. Smaller—yet still potentially catastrophic—asteroids impact the planet far more frequently. The Spaceguard Survey projects that asteroids 200 meters (656 feet) in diameter strike the earth at intervals of 5,000 years, and asteroids 500 meters across (1,640 feet) hit at 40,000-year intervals. Whatever the interval, there is no question that asteroids of various sizes have struck the earth hundreds if not thousands of times over the 4.6 billion years that our planet has existed.

Perhaps even more frightening than the frequency of asteroid impacts is the fact that—even with all our telescopes, distant sensing devices, and other modern technology—we still have no way of predicting when the next asteroid will career in from space, or being certain of detecting it when it inevitably does.

While the ocean impact of an asteroid one kilometer in diameter would undoubtedly take a high toll of human lives and wreak havoc on surrounding coastlines, the catastrophe would pale in comparison to the devastation that swept the world in the aftermath of the asteroid that struck the earth at the end of the Cretaceous period, wiping out the dinosaurs and 76 percent of all the other animals and plants on the planet. That asteroid—estimated to be the size of Mount Everest—struck the coast of Yucatan on the Gulf of Mexico with a velocity of 20 miles per second, 100 times faster than the speed of a bullet.

The impact vaporized both the water and the seabed below, creating a crater 60 miles in diameter and 20 miles deep. The incredible energy released by the strike spawned a tsunami that towered hundreds or perhaps even thousands of feet high. After devastating the islands and coasts of the Gulf of Mexico—there is evidence that the tsunami may have submerged the entire Florida peninsula and surged as far inland as northern Alabama—the giant wave circled the earth several times, drowning the lands lying near the sea and leaving only the interiors of the continents unscathed.

Whether the next mega-tsunami is caused by an earthquake, a submarine landslide, a volcanic eruption, or an asteroid impact, when the huge wave reaches land it will take uncounted lives, and leave almost every human on the planet psychologically scarred. Imagine looking out the window of your office on the 50th floor of a skyscraper in lower Manhattan and seeing a wave racing in from the Atlantic that is cresting 200 feet above the top of your building. Envision driving across the Golden Gate Bridge with your wife or husband when she or he suddenly screams and points to a tsunami higher than the roadway, 10 seconds away from washing your car into the roiling bay. Could there be anything more horrifying than staring up at a sky-high wall of water and knowing that you have no time to flee, no way to escape a watery death?

Another mega-tsunami is on the way, and there will be nothing humans can do to stop it. If you live on or near an ocean coast, you may see such a monster wave in your lifetime. And it will be the last thing you see.

PLAGUES

A guest was found dead in Room 8-H of Miami Beach's posh Eden Blue Hotel. This in itself was not unusual in the Sunshine State, with its high proportion of elderly residents and visitors. What was unusual was the manner of death.

A stench that the closed door could not contain prompted a chambermaid to ignore the "Do Not Disturb" sign and use her key to unlock the door. She took a few steps into the room and froze as she took in the full horror of the scene.

A man lay sprawled across the unmade bed, tangled in the sheets, drenched in gore. Blood was everywhere. The suite looked like a slaughterhouse.

Overcoming her paralysis, the chambermaid backed out of the room and into the hall, carefully secured the door behind her, and ran at top speed to notify the shift supervisor.

Miami Police Department homicide detectives and crime-scene technicians were soon swarming the hotel. Even veteran investigators were impressed by the ghastliness of the scene. Blood seemed to have issued from everywhere on the victim's body: eyes, nose, ears, mouth, and other orifices. Less obvious was the cause of death; the amount of blood made it impossible even with careful scrutiny to detect any fatal wounds such as bullet holes or slash marks. Detectives called such evident violence "overkill," a frequent hallmark of drug-related homicides.

Crime-scene technicians moved through the hotel suite, photographing it from various angles, collecting specimens and samples, bagging and tagging potential evidence. The threat of AIDS and other blood-borne diseases and the dangers of contaminating the evidence had long ago caused forensics personnel to develop protocols for handling such incidents. From the neck down, the technicians wore surgical scrubs, latex gloves, and plastic bags over their shoes (to avoid tracking in extraneous materials). After the scene had been processed, personnel from the medical examiner's department secured the corpse in a body bag and took it to the morgue. Bloody sheets, bedclothes, towels, and garments were transported to the police department's evidence lockers.

Investigators learned that the dead man was middle-aged, a native of Holland, and an international diamond dealer. The diamond connection piqued the interest of the sleuths, since valuable jewels could certainly supply a motive for what they assumed was a murder, and most likely a torture-murder. They began following up leads, digging into the victim's background and recent past.

The spectacular nature of the case made it a top priority, causing the post-mortem examination to be scheduled as early as possible, within 24 hours. Present were the assistant medical examiner, his assistant, and several orderlies. Also present were some MPD homicide detectives handling the case of the deceased diamond merchant. Standard procedure called for the cadaver to be examined, anomalies noted, blood and other bodily fluid samples taken, and internal organs weighed and dissected.

The corpse was laid out on a steel examining table while the forensic pathologists grouped around it—but the examination ended almost before it began. One of the pathologists, seeing the body for the first time and noting its condition, immediately suspected that the cause of death was not so much homicidal as epidemiological. It was a major case, all right— a major case of plague.

Near-panic erupted in the autopsy room as police and morgue staff stampeded for the doors. Finally, the assistant M.E. restored order, sealing the immediate area under quarantine to await the arrival of a team of doctors from the nearest branch of the Center for Disease Control. Medical and police personnel present at the autopsy were sequestered at the morgue. Their fear deepened when the CDC team arrived outfitted head to toe in white protective suits complete with their own air supplies.

The CDC team examined the corpse and quickly identified the killer: the Ebola virus. The diamond dealer had succumbed to hemorrhagic fever transmitted from the virus, causing him to spill blood from all orifices, including the pores of his skin. His internal organs had literally been turned to mush.

Subsequent investigation revealed that the deceased had been with a group of international gem merchants who had recently gathered in the African nation of Sierra Leone to attend an auction of uncut diamonds. The diamonds came from mines in the Congo, and were being sold by representatives of a Congolese rebel group operating in the provinces outside Katanga. This was a fairly common practice, done by the rebel groups to raise money to buy weapons. Such gems are commonly known as "blood diamonds," due to the violent means by which they reach the international market. This time, though, the gems being auctioned off really *were* blood diamonds: Their handlers were carrying the Ebola virus.

Ebola virus flourishes deep in the jungle, in remote places normally shunned by humans, in caves and coverts—the same places frequented by the rebel groups, who use them as hideouts and bases from which to prosecute their war against the Katanga government. Somewhere, in a cave used by the rebels, the Ebola virus lurked, perhaps buried below the muck sliming the cave floor. The opportunistic virus attached itself to these obliging hosts. This first generation had an incubation period of two to three weeks. Not knowing that they were infected, the rebels had moved on.

Remaining in Sierra Leone for a few days afterward to finalize his transactions, the dealer then flew to Miami for a series of meetings with gem brokers from the big South American markets. Finally, the disease blossomed within him, brutally striking him down in his hotel room. Too weak to phone for help, he'd finally expired. The Ebola strain that killed the diamond dealer had incubated in 10 days. This meant that a particularly virulent strain was potentiating now that it was loose in the general population. Ebola had arrived. The virus spread through casual contact with the infected, even though they might show no outward signs of the disease. And direct contact was not required. A healthy person could pick up the virus by touching a doorknob that had previously been touched by a carrier. Those who'd ridden on the same plane out of Sierra Leone taken by the dealer were at risk. Everyone he'd encountered at Miami airport was at risk. Some of the contaminated then boarded planes for other destinations, vectoring the disease in all directions. The South American brokers with whom the dealer met in Miami took the virus home with them. The diamond dealer had also been entertained by several female escorts who, after intimate contact with the doomed man, entertained numerous other sexual partners before the Ebola felled them. Those partners passed the virus to their partners, in ever-expanding circles of contamination and doom.

Even as the Miami authorities wrestled with how to contain the galloping plague without triggering a mad panic, the first victims were already turning up at local hospitals. Complicating the containment effort was the fact that medical personnel who treated Ebola victims were themselves at ultra-high risk for catching the disease. How would doctors and nurses react once they learned the true nature of the bloody malady afflicting the infected? How would the city react to the knowledge that a deadly plague was astir in the bloodstream of its own populace?

And of course, there had been many others at the meeting in Sierra Leone. A geometrically expanding progression of contamination was now spreading inexorably throughout the hemisphere and worldwide, and the dying had already begun.

No war, no natural catastrophe, no famine, no blood-soaked reign of a terrible tyrant so decimated the world's population as did the fourteenth-century outbreak of bubonic plague known as the Black Death. Twenty-five million Europeans—a quarter to half the population of the continent—died in the span of five years. Uncounted millions more perished in Asia and North Africa, and trade and commerce virtually came to a halt.

The epidemic that swept the civilized world in the 1330s began in China, and soon spread to western Asia and then to Europe. History tells us that the disease arrived in Europe aboard Italian merchant ships that docked in Sicily after crossing the eastern Mediterranean from the Black Sea laden with Chinese trade goods. When the ships pulled into harbor, many of the sailors were already dying of the plague. Within days, the disease had spread through the port like wildfire, and Sicilians began dying in droves. An eyewitness wrote, "Realizing what a deadly disaster had come to them, the people quickly drove the Italians from their city. But the disease remained, and soon death was everywhere. Fathers abandoned their sick sons. Lawyers refused to come and make out wills for the dying. Friars and nuns were left to care for the sick, and monasteries and convents were soon deserted, as they were stricken, too. Bodies were left in empty houses, and there was no one to give them a Christian burial."

The Black Death killed people with terrifying speed. As the fourteenth-century Italian writer Boccaccio recounts, "Victims often ate lunch with their friends, and dinner with their ancestors in paradise."

In many cities and towns, the dead outnumbered the living, and rotting corpses littered the streets. Bodies were often simply tossed into shallow mass graves, and domesticated cats and dogs—starving after being abandoned by their owners—dug up the dead to eat.

What evil force could have visited such widespread death upon humanity? Was the disease carried around the known world by a marauding horde like the Visigoths, the Huns, or the Mongols? Did global famine trigger the pandemic? Was it an act of God foretold in the Judeo-Christian scriptures? As it turns out, the agent of doom was an insect smaller than a grain of rice. The murderer of millions was a flea. A female flea, to be exact; its scientific name is *Xenopsylla cheopsis*, in the order *Siphonaptera*. Otherwise known as the rat flea, only the adult females of the species feed on hosts. The bubonic plague was spread when the fleas drank the blood of rats carrying the plague bacteria. When these same fleas later bit people, they regurgitated bacteria-laced rat blood into the wound, infecting humans.

Deadly diseases are lurking out there, waiting to mushroom into a worldwide epidemic. A modern plague could race around the world in days because of the speed of modern transportation.

Why would accounts of the Black Death be relevant in the modern world? The answer lies in the simple truism, "Those who cannot remember the past are condemned to repeat it." Deadly diseases are lurking out there—some of them presently unknown to science—waiting for the right conditions to mushroom into a worldwide epidemic. While the Black Death took several years to spread from China to Europe, a modern plague could race around the world in weeks or even days because of the speed of modern transportation, especially planes, and the ever-increasing frequency with which people from different countries and continents intermingle.

THE KILLERS AMONG US

The killer viruses that pose the greatest danger today include AIDS, hemorrhagic fevers like Ebola, super-viruses, encephalitis, smallpox, and new strains of influenza. Life-threatening diseases caused by bacteria rather than viruses include various forms of plague, cholera, botulism, Legionnaire's Disease, Meningitis, relapsing fever, anthrax, tuberculosis, and flesh-eating bacteria. Diseases—notably typhus—caused by microorganisms classified between viruses and bacteria are known as rickettsias. There are also major diseases that are spread through causative agents other than viruses or bacteria. Malaria, for instance, is caused by single-celled parasites. In the case of Mad Cow Disease, the transmissible agent is a newly discovered pathogen called a *prion*, short for "proteinaceous infectious particle." There are undoubtedly other lethal viruses, bacteria, parasites, and prions capable of killing millions—or even causing the extinction of the entire human species—that have yet to emerge from some remote swamp or jungle, and remain unknown to humanity.

An individual infected with one of these deadly new diseases—or a lethal mutation of an existing disease—could fly from his or her homeland to Europe or the United States in a matter of hours. If that person's destination were a large city like London or New York, the infection could spread to tens or even hundreds of thousands within a few days. Since there would be no viable vaccines to treat the previously unknown infection, the death toll from the outbreak of a new disease would be staggering.

One has only to consider the pandemic spread of AIDS in recent years to understand the human devastation that would accompany the release of an untreatable killer disease upon the world. AIDS is thought to be caused by exposure to the Human Immunodeficiency Virus (HIV). The disease was virtually unknown before 1981, when the first cases were reported in the United States. Subsequent research has turned up evidence of HIV infection in a plasma sample taken from an adult male in central Africa in 1959, in tissue samples taken from a black teenager who died in Missouri in 1969, and in tissue samples from a Norwegian sailor who died in 1976. Scientists now generally agree that HIV evolved from simian (monkey) immunodeficiency virus (SIV). It is still not known for certain how HIV crossed species, although it has long been accepted that certain viruses can be transferred from animals to humans in a process called zoonosis. Researchers at the University of Alabama have put forward a theory that HIV could have passed from chimpanzees to humans when an African hunter killed and ate a chimp.

Whatever the origins of AIDS, the disease spread rapidly, especially among gay men, hemophiliacs, and intravenous drug users. By the end of 1984, 7,000 Americans had AIDS, and thousands of other cases were reported around the world. Within 12 months the disease had spread to 51 countries, and in the years that followed, the AIDS outbreak mushroomed into a global plague that infected tens of millions of men, women, and children in almost every country on earth.

Several months after the September 11 terrorist attack on the World Trade Center, former president Bill Clinton delivered the Diana, Princess of Wales, Memorial Lecture for the National AIDS Trust in London. In an impassioned speech, Clinton told the audience that the AIDS epidemic ravaging Africa and spreading fast in eastern Europe and the Caribbean is a bigger potential threat to the peace and prosperity of the world than global terrorism. "There are now forty million people living with AIDS," he said. "The number is projected to rise to one hundred million by 2005. If that happens, it probably will be enough to crumble fledgling democracies. It probably will be enough to spread violence among young people who fear that they only have a year or so to live and therefore can't understand why they shouldn't be involved in whatever conflict is handy."

Clinton warned that AIDS is potentially the most catastrophic plague the world has faced since the Black Death devastated Europe in the fourteenth century, and noted pointedly that to date the United States and the United Kingdom have contributed only a few million dollars toward their share of the annual $10 billion UN global fund for HIV/AIDS, TB, and malaria.

One hundred million people infected with AIDS! And there is still no cure in sight! On the contrary, medicines now used to treat the disease are becoming less and less effective. A recent nationwide study discovered that at least one major drug used for the treatment of AIDS no longer works, and that 78 percent of Americans being treated for HIV infection carry a virus that is already resistant to one or more anti-HIV drugs.

"It does mean patients are running out of options," says study co-leader Samuel A. Bozzette, M.D., Ph.D., a researcher at the University of California, San Diego, and the VA San Diego Healthcare System. "Treatment of HIV is going to be increasingly complicated."

The implications of the study are dire indeed, not only for the 100 million or more people who will soon be infected with AIDS but for the future of entire countries, if not continents. When the Black Death killed tens of millions in Europe during the Middle Ages, trade and commerce came to a screeching halt, food production fell because of a lack of farm workers, governments collapsed, and society teetered on the brink of anarchy. Does the same fate await Eastern Europe, the Caribbean, and much of Africa? With AIDS spreading unchecked, no cure in sight, and existing drug treatments becoming less and less effective, it's hard to see any future for these HIV-infested regions other than decades of death, devastation, and despair.

THE NIGHTMARE OF EBOLA

There is a second deadly virus indigenous to Africa that causes not only a far faster but also a far more horrible death than AIDS. The disease is called Ebola. In an article for *Scientific American*, Gunjan Sinha and Corey S. Powell wrote, "If one were to rank the world's most gruesome ways to die, Ebola infection would surely sit near the top of the list. It begins with a sudden fever and then kills by liquefying peoples' insides."

Up to 90 percent of the people who contract Ebola die, making the disease one of the most deadly viruses ever to afflict humans. Another disturbing element of Ebola is that we know so little about it, mainly because it is a pathogen that until relatively recently was unknown to us.

One mysterious aspect of the disease is where it comes from. It is not known whether the "reservoir host"—an animal or arthropod involved in the life cycle of the virus—is a monkey, another mammal, a bird, a reptile, a mosquito, a tick, or some other creature. According to the article by Sinha and Powell, scientists from the Centers for Disease Control (CDC), the World Health Organization, and the U.S. Army are currently screening hundreds of African animal species in search of the reservoir. The current belief is that the animal is either widespread in central Africa, or else a migratory species.

Dr. Lindsey Martinez, quoted in a news article written by CNN correspondent Jim Clancy, said that no one knows where Ebola hides in between epidemics. "And the investigations are still going on, looking at the animal reservoir to try and find which animal or insect may be harboring the virus and enabling it to re-emerge from time to time."

It's a pretty good bet that there are other previously unknown diseases out there somewhere, waiting to suddenly emerge as Ebola did. As advanced as science and medicine have become, there is no way we can come up with an instant cure for a disease we have never encountered before.

It is not just the mystery of Ebola but also its ferocity that sets it apart from other diseases. The virulence of the virus sends shudders down the spines of even seasoned researchers. Victims first experience severe headache and begin burning up with a searing fever. Then their throats and the mucous membranes of their eyes become inflamed. At the same time they begin to vomit uncontrollably and suffer violent spasms of diarrhea. Then the bleeding begins. Blood gushes out through the eyes, lips, nose, ears, vagina, penis, rectum, and skin. After about five days of infection, the victim's internal organs turn into mush and a horrible death soon follows.

Jim Clancy described the effects of the disease even more graphically in his piece for CNN. "Ebola virus victims usually 'crash and bleed,' a military term which literally means the virus attacks every organ of the body and transforms every part of the body into a digested slime of virus particles."

Named after the Ebola River in the Democratic Republic of the Congo in central Africa, the disease was formally known as Ebola hemorrhagic fever, and is one of two members of a family of ribonucleic acid (RNA) viruses called the filoviridae. Only one person has reportedly become infected in the United States; the disease most commonly strikes Africans. Confirmed cases have been reported in the Congo, Gabon, Sudan, the Ivory Coast, and Uganda. Since Ebola was first recognized in 1976, four species of the disease have been identified: Ebola-Zaire, Ebola-Sudan, Ebola-Ivory Coast, and Ebola-Reston. The first three species can transmit the virus to humans, while Ebola-Reston only infects nonhuman primates.

Ebola is incredibly infectious and can transmit easily from person to person through close contact. The disease leaves cells on an infected person's skin, and if another person touches the victim's skin and then touches an opening on his or her own body, such as the mouth, that person will become infected. Ebola can also be transmitted through body fluids such as blood, vomit, secretions, or semen. Even people who come into only fleeting contact with these fluids—such as doctors, nurses, and other medical personnel—run a high risk of becoming infected. The disease can also spread through the sharing of hypodermic needles.

Ebola typically takes effect 2 to 21 days after a person has contracted the virus. The timeline depends largely on whether a person suffered a direct infection, such as from a hypodermic needle, or an indirect infection through close contact. The time it takes for symptoms to appear raises the scary possibility that a person could be infected with Ebola, get on a plane, and be on the other side of the world before the disease broke out. It is entirely possible that a great many of the Ebola victim's fellow passengers, as well as the plane's crew, would contract the disease, as would scores of people the infected person comes in contact with at his or her destination.

> A person could be infected with Ebola, get on a plane, and be on the other side of the world before the disease broke out.

We know this can happen because the disease has already traveled by air from continent to continent, not within the bodies of infected humans but in the blood of primates. Two shipments of monkeys exported from the Philippines to the United States carried the Ebola virus with them. Fortunately, the species of disease involved was Ebola-Reston, a strain that so far is only fatal to nonhumans. In 1989, the first shipment of infected monkeys spread the virus through a primate research facility in Reston, Virginia—where it acquired its name—and seven years later the second shipment infected a primate center in Alice, Texas. Both outbreaks spread fear—if not panic—among scientists and civilians alike, and brought drastic action from authorities. In Reston, all the monkeys in the research facilities were euthanized, and the building where they'd been caged was sealed off with airtight tape and guarded around the clock to keep the unwary away.

Why take such extreme precautions against a species of Ebola that is only known to infect nonhumans? Correspondent Jeff Levine answered the question in a news piece for CNN. "Just because Ebola-Reston doesn't hurt humans now doesn't mean it can't change. In the 20 years since scientists first encountered the Ebola virus, they have learned much about its extraordinary ability to mutate into different forms. 'Because it can mutate,' said Gerald Stokes of George Washington University, 'even benign forms of Ebola have the potential to become fatal to humans. Any virus that has the ability to change or mutate, theoretically has the possibility of becoming virulent—that is a concern.'"

Levine quotes Dr. Peter Jahrling of the U.S. Army speaking after the Reston outbreak. "'My concern has always been that when we encounter a virus as we have now, folks will let their guard down and say, Oh, it's just Ebola-Reston; it's not a problem. It is a problem.'"

With no known cure and a mortality rate of up to 90 percent, Ebola is not just a problem but a global catastrophe waiting to happen. If the virus should suddenly migrate from the remote regions of Africa to heavily populated parts of the world, the highly contagious disease could threaten the very existence of human life on this planet.

MAD WITH FEVERS

Although Ebola is undoubtedly the most deadly of the group of viral diseases known as hemorrhagic fevers, there are several other viruses that can also cause severe illness and death. These include hantavirus, lassa fever, yellow fever, and Dengue fever.

Hantavirus is a genus of viruses carried by mice, rats, and voles. During the Korean War, hantavirus caused a bleeding disease—or hemorrhagic fever—that infected more than 2,500 U.S. soldiers and killed as many as 250 of them. For 40 years after the war, the disease disappeared from the medical radar scope. Then, in 1993, the virus reappeared with a vengeance in the Four Corners area of the American Southwest. Fifty-three people became infected, and an astounding 32 of these died. The Center for Disease Control identified the disease a month after the outbreak began and named it the Sin Nombre (no name) virus. The Sin Nombre species of hantavirus is up to 10 times deadlier than the virus that struck in Korea. This fact begs the question: Is there an even more lethal strain of hantavirus out there somewhere in the world, and—if so—when will the next outbreak come, and how many will it kill?

This group of viruses also includes Dengue fever and Dengue hemorrhagic fever (DHF). Dengue fever is a flu-like illness, while DHF is a severe complication of Dengue fever which can cause a sudden onset of muscle and joint pain, fever, bleeding, shock from loss of blood, and death. The Centers for Disease Control report that Dengue and DHF are caused by, "one of four closely related, but antigenically distinct, virus stereotypes (DEN-1, DEN-2, DEN-3 and DEN-4), of the genus *Flavivirus*."

Dengue fever is the most widespread mosquito-borne viral disease affecting humans. People are most often infected with the disease when they are bitten by a mosquito with the scientific name *Aedes aegypti*. The mosquito bites during the day, and prefers to feed on humans. The virus is known to have existed in the tropical regions of Asia, Africa, and the Americas for the past 200 years, and today an estimated 2.5 billion people live in areas at risk for Dengue epidemics. Tens of millions of people are infected with Dengue fever each year, and hundreds of thousands more become victims of DHF. Even the public health-conscious United States is not immune to the disease. Several thousand known or suspected cases of Dengue fever have been reported in recent years, and the southern states are constantly at risk that a Dengue epidemic will break out.

One of the most disturbing things about Dengue is how rapidly it is spreading around the world. According to the Centers for Disease Control, "… the geographic distribution of dengue viruses and their mosquito vectors has expanded, and DHF has emerged in the Pacific region and the Americas. In Southeast Asia, epidemic DHF first appeared in the 1950s, but by 1975 it had become a leading cause of hospitalization and death among children in many countries in that region. In the 1980s, DHF began a second expansion into Asia when Sri Lanka, India, and the Maldive Islands had their first major DHF epidemics. Pakistan first reported an epidemic of dengue fever in 1994."

The CDC report lists epidemics of DHF on several Pacific islands, in Africa, and in the Caribbean and Central America. By the dawning of the third millennia, virtually every tropical country on Earth had suffered through a Dengue epidemic. The reasons for the dramatic global emergence of Dengue/DHF are complex, but the CDC focuses on three main causes. "First, effective mosquito control is virtually nonexistent in most dengue-endemic countries. Considerable emphasis for the past 20 years has been placed on ultra-low-volume insecticide space sprays for adult mosquito control, a relatively ineffective approach for controlling Ae. Aegypti.

"Second, major global demographic changes have occurred, the most important of which have been uncontrolled urbanization and concurrent population growth. These demographic changes have resulted in substandard housing and in adequate water, sewer, and waste management systems, all of which increase Ae. aegypti population densities and facilitate transmission of Ae. aegypti-borne disease."

Are you beginning to get an inkling that maybe the rapid spread of disease so common in the world today is not a "natural" phenomenon? Read on.

The third reason for recent epidemics of Dengue, the CDC reports, is that, "… increased travel by airplane provides the ideal mechanism for transporting dengue viruses between population centers of the tropics, resulting in a constant exchange of dengue viruses and other pathogens."

In other words, just as with AIDS and Ebola, the spread of Dengue fever is being facilitated by a combination of modern technology and the unwise actions of humans. Not only are we failing to control the carriers of disease such as rodents and mosquitoes—and being careless with how we handle lab monkeys that may be infected—we're also providing potentially lethal insects with ideal breeding and feeding grounds and flying monkeys contaminated with the Ebola virus into primate centers a stone's throw from heavily populated areas.

Lassa fever is another of the hemorrhagic fevers that originated in Africa. Like Ebola, today the disease is found primarily in west Africa. The virus's symptoms are high fever, mouth ulcers, muscle aches, and bleeding through the skin. The virus is spread via the Mastomys rat and transmitted to humans when the rat's urine contaminates food or invades a person's body in the form of airborne droplets. According to the *Columbia Encyclopedia*, "The incubation period of Lassa fever is three to seven days. Following fever and general malaise, later stages of the disease may include abdominal pain, diarrhea, vomiting, and petechiae, tiny purplish spots in the skin caused by leakage of blood from the capillaries. Heart and kidney failure may also occur in advanced stages, and the mortality is high, ranging about 25 to 30 percent."

While Lassa fever is presently confined to west Africa, and remains relatively obscure, that could change tomorrow if the disease mutates, finds a new host, and invades the heavily populated northern hemisphere.

Yellow fever is perhaps the best known of major hemorrhagic fevers because of the infamous role it played in the construction of the Panama Canal. The disease was one of the primary reasons that the French failed in their effort to build a canal across Panama, and it had to be controlled before the Americans could succeed in linking the Atlantic and Pacific. The virus is spread by the bite of the female *Aedes aegypti* mosquito, the same mosquito that transmits Dengue fever. The insect typically breeds in stagnant water near human habitations.

Yellow fever has an incubation period of three to five days. Although the disease may cause only fever and headache in less severe cases, the more virulent form of the virus can also produce chills, rapid heartbeat, bleeding into the skin, and paralyzing prostration. Within three days, the victim is usually stricken with jaundice. Thereafter, the symptoms commonly lessen, but soon return with renewed violence. In the final stage of the disease the patient may suffer internal hemorrhaging, delirium, and coma. In the most severe cases, the disease is fatal.

All hemorrhagic fevers have a high mortality rate, but it is truly mind-numbing to know that 85 out of 100 people who are infected with yellow fever are going to die if left untreated, which will likely be the case for victims of the virus who live in the poor, medically backward countries of the tropics. How would you like those odds the next time you get sick?

The Marburg virus, yet another hemorrhagic fever, first struck in 1967 at a vaccine factory in Marburg, Germany. Three employees became ill with what they thought was the flu. Within 24 hours, their condition had worsened and they soon began to suffer diarrhea, bloody vomiting, and hemorrhaging from every orifice. To the horror of the victims and their caregivers, their skin came off. During the course of the outbreak of Marburg virus, more than 30 doctors, technicians, and family members of the victims became infected in Germany and Yugoslavia. When the crisis had passed, seven people were dead and scores of others suffered liver damage, impotence, and psychosis. The disease was traced to exposure to a shipment of African green monkeys from Uganda, a scenario very similar to the later outbreaks of Ebola-Reston in Virginia and Texas, except that in this case humans were infected.

> To the horror of the victims and their caregivers, their skin came off.

Rift Valley fever (RVF)—a virus that primarily infects domestic animals in Africa such as cattle, buffalo, sheep, goats, and camels—will occasionally progress to hemorrhagic fever in humans. Found primarily in eastern and southern Africa, the disease is transmitted by the bites of mosquitoes carrying the virus. People can also be infected by exposure to the blood or body fluids of infected animals. The CDC reports that, "There is no established course of treatment for patients infected with RVF virus. However, studies in monkeys and other animals have shown promise for ribavirin, an antiviral drug, for future use in humans."

Although all these viruses can—and obviously often do—kill people, and sometimes cause localized epidemics, their greatest threat is that they will mutate into an even more lethal species. Given the extraordinary ability of viruses to change, there is little doubt that mutations will appear sometime in the future. What form the new species will take, how lethal the viruses will be, and how fast they will spread, no one knows. And that may be the scariest part of all.

A NEW FLU?

Although newly discovered exotic viruses such as hemorrhagic fevers may someday threaten our very existence, we are also in danger of becoming too complacent about more familiar pandemic diseases that could suddenly mutate and wipe out tens of millions. Influenza is a prime example. The flu is a contagious virus whose symptoms include fever, headache, extreme tiredness, dry cough, sore throat, nasal congestion, and body aches. According to the CDC, 10 to 20 percent of U.S. residents will get the flu each year, and 20,000 will die from the disease. Another 114,000 will have to be admitted to the hospital.

"The flu is spread, or transmitted, when a person who has the flu coughs, sneezes, or speaks, and sends flu virus into the air, and other people inhale the virus," the CDC report tells us. "The virus enters the nose, throat, or lungs of a person and begins to multiply, causing symptoms of the flu. Flu may, less often, be spread when a person touches a surface that has flu viruses on it—a door handle, for instance—and then touches his or her nose or mouth."

Almost everyone has had the flu at one time or another. Although the disease is certainly not pleasant to have to go through, most people recover in a week or two, and few of us consider the virus life-threatening. But it is. Indeed, in the past century alone, flu has killed more people than did the Black Death. The worst outbreak of the disease came in 1918 when the Spanish Flu pandemic swept the world, infecting an incredible 525 million people and killing 40 million of them.

The virus originated in Tibet in 1917 but soon spread to India, China, and Europe. For reasons that are still unknown, when the disease reached

France and began infecting African soldiers serving in the French Army, the virus strain suddenly mutated and became even more deadly.

Leonard Crane, author of *The Ninth Day of Creation*, writes that, "By the fall of 1918, a strain of influenza seemingly no different from that of previous years suddenly turned so deadly, and engendered such a state of panic and chaos in communities across the globe, that many people believed the world was coming to an end."

The virus took lives more quickly than almost any other disease ever known, often killing people within only hours of the first indication of infection. Thousands of American soldiers serving in the First World War contracted the disease and brought it home with them when the war was over. All over the country, the joyous reunions of doughboys with their families turned to scenes of anguish as both the soldiers and their loved ones fell victim to the virulent virus. It's estimated that 675,000 Americans died from the Spanish flu between 1918 and 1919, with almost 200,000 perishing in the month of October 1918 alone. Even today you can go through cemeteries in different parts of the country and find gravestones carved with inscriptions bearing sad witness to the annihilation of entire families by the disease.

Crane adds this ominous prediction about future outbreaks of flu: "With the world population today having more than tripled in the intervening years [since 40 million died from the Spanish flu], what is to stop a modern flu pandemic from claiming upward of 100 million lives? The answer, it seems, is nothing at all."

An unusual aspect of the Spanish flu was that most of its victims were people in the prime of their lives rather than the more vulnerable young and old, the usual target of communicable diseases. Scientists still don't know why the virus primarily infected healthy, vigorous people, but the fact that it did bodes ill for civilization when the next outbreak comes. The people from 20 to 50 years old that the disease targeted are the same people who manage and maintain the infrastructure of our daily lives: communications, manufacturing, transportation, finance, food and fuel distribution, and so on. If millions of our best and brightest suddenly die—leaving a gaping void in a critical segment of the workforce—our society could crumble into chaos.

CHAPTER 7: PLAGUES

There are those who will argue that such a dire scenario will never come about because we now have influenza vaccines, and all that people have to do to prevent contracting the virus is to get a flu shot. The problem is that while a vaccination may protect you from known strains of the flu, all the shots in the world will do you no good if you're exposed to a new species of the disease.

In late 1997, just such a new strain of flu virus suddenly appeared in Hong Kong, CNN Correspondent Donna Liu teamed up with the Reuters news service to report the story: "Hong Kong health officials on Monday began stalking a 'bird flu' virus suspected of killing two people in the territory and sickening two others, and called for international assistance in developing a vaccine against the disease."

The new strain of influenza virus was identified as H5N1, a disease that before that time was thought to be confined to poultry. Health officials—including the United Nations World Health Organization (WHO)—scrambled to produce a vaccine to treat the virus before it could spread. The primary danger was that humans had no immunity to the new strain of flu—one of several known viruses that had crossed over to humans after first infecting animals—and the relative handful of cases in Hong Kong could mushroom into a worldwide epidemic.

Dr. Robert Wagner, chairman of the Department of Virology and Molecular Biology at Saint Jude Children's Research Hospital in Memphis, came out with this chilling observation in the book *The Invisible Invaders* by Peter Radetsky. "All the genes of influenza viruses in the world are being maintained in aquatic birds, and periodically they transmit to other species. The 1918 viruses are still being maintained in the bird reservoir. So even though these viruses are very ancient, they still have the capacity to evolve, to acquire new genes, new hosts. *The potential is still there for the catastrophe of 1918 to happen again.*" (Italics added.)

Will the next case of flu you get be a relatively benign strain that will only put you in bed for a few days, or will it be a virulent new species that will put you in your grave? No one knows.

THE SMALLPOX BOMB

While influenza remains a potent disease, the once-universally feared smallpox virus has been purged from the world. Right? Well, yes and no. Scientists estimate that over its 3,000 year history, smallpox has taken 100 million lives and left another 200 million people blind and scarred. The Spanish brought smallpox with them when they settled in Hispaniola in 1509, and by 1518 every single one of the island's original Native American inhabitants was dead of the disease. In the American colonies during the seventeenth and eighteenth centuries, smallpox killed 90 percent of the people who became infected.

Before WHO launched a vaccine drive to eradicate the disease in 1967, the disease was still killing two million people a year worldwide. The last known case of the virus was reported in 1977.

The world rejoiced that the often-fatal infection had been eradicated—except in two places: the laboratories of the Centers for Disease Control in Atlanta, Georgia, and the Russian State Centre for Research on Virology and Biotechnology in Koltsovo, Russian Federation.

There might also be one other place—a yet-unknown terrorist camp in Somalia, Yemen, Indonesia, or the Philippines. Western intelligence has long suspected that unpaid or unemployed Russian researchers—bracketed by their starving families on one side and a lax laboratory security system on the other—may have sold smallpox virus, and perhaps their own services, to well-financed terrorist groups like Osama bin Laden's al Qaeda. If this has indeed happened, then the world faces a far more insidious and lethal threat than suicidal terrorists hijacking more planes and crashing them into our urban skyscrapers. The widespread death that drew a dark shroud over the world for so many centuries could reappear if a terrorist-sponsored scientist were to succeed in producing a more virulent strain of smallpox and the disease were set loose in a large American or European city.

A new smallpox pandemic could also sweep the world if the disease should undergo a natural permutation into a strain of the virus for which no vaccine presently exists. This danger is especially acute in overcrowded countries with inadequate medical personnel, such as India, where the new disease could infect hundreds of thousands or even millions before the symptoms were recognized.

Perhaps the most publicized health menace in recent years has been Mad Cow Disease, which is also known as BSE, for bovine spongiform encephalopathy, a scientific term that reflects the spongy appearance of an infected brain. The human form of the infection is called Creutzfeld-Jakob Disease (CJD). It is thought that cattle contract Mad Cow Disease from eating feed containing meat and bone contaminated with scrapie, a fatal degenerative disease found in sheep and goats. BSE damages the brain, spinal cord, and central nervous system of cattle, bringing on neurological disease that manifests itself in changes in temperament, lack of coordination, difficulty rising, and unexplained weight loss.

Most scientists now believe that people can get vCJD, a variant of Creutzfeld-Jakob disease, from eating mad cows. According to The Why Files, an internet information resource provided by the University of Wisconsin, "While CJD mainly affects the elderly, vCJD appears among younger people, almost certainly from eating mad cow meat. The gruesome death starts with mood swings, numbness, and uncontrolled body movements. Eventually the mind is destroyed, somewhat like Alzheimer's, another brain wrecking disease. The newer variety of CJD usually kills in about 18 months after symptoms appear, compared to four to six months for regular CJD. *There is no treatment, and both diseases are uniformly fatal.*" (Italics added.)

As of the writing of this book, Europe, especially Britain, has borne the brunt of the Mad Cow Disease epidemic. Only 70 to 100 people have been known to die so far from vCJD contracted by eating the meat of infected cattle, but that figure will undoubtedly increase in the years and decades to come. Britain's *Guardian Newspapers* recently carried a story on their website that projected ominous estimates of the possible death toll from Mad Cow disease. "… Scientists said CJD would ultimately claim 136,000 lives, a much smaller number than previous estimates. At one point there seemed to be no limit to the numbers potentially at risk. *A European committee thought that a single animal with BSE could put up to 500,000 people at risk.*" (Italics added.)

Fortunately, the United States has so far been immune from Mad Cow disease. No cattle here have tested positive for BSE, and—although at least 200 Americans a year are diagnosed with CJD—none of these cases have been linked to eating meat infected with Mad Cow disease. We're home free! Unless, of course, you put credence in the findings of former U.S. Surgeon General C. Everett Koop, who estimates that 95 percent of Americans have Mad Cow Disease parasites in their bodies from eating meat products and fish. Koop and many other scientists believe that the disease has an incubation period of three to nine years, which means that uncounted people who show no signs of the malady now will someday die of CJD.

Perhaps the most horrific disease humans may contract is Necrotizing Fasciitis/Myositis—better known as flesh-eating disease. This is—for now—a rare disease in which bacteria eat away a person's flesh faster than a surgeon could cut it out with a scalpel. The causative agent is a strain of *Streptococcus pyogenes*, and the disease is spread when droplets of saliva or nasal secretions pass from person to person. The bacteria basically eat a victim alive, and patients must endure the unspeakable agony of lying in hospital beds watching their flesh vanish before their eyes.

Legionnaire's Disease (LD) is yet another epidemic waiting to happen. The illness is a form of pneumonia, and is caused by exposure to the bacterium *Legionella pneumophila*. The disease got its name when scores of legionnaires attending an American Legion convention in Philadelphia in 1976 came down with pneumonia. People usually contract the disease after breathing mist that comes from a warm, stagnant water source such as an air-conditioning-cooling tower, a whirlpool spa, or a shower drawing water from a seldom-used hot-water heater. Up to 18,000 people a year contract Legionnaires' Disease in the United States. Although only a relatively small percentage of those stricken die, if the bacteria should change into a more lethal strain, the widespread use of warm water in homes, office buildings, recreational facilities, and factories could send the death toll into the stratosphere.

Before the fall of 2001, most people thought of anthrax—if they thought of it at all—as a disease relegated to hoofed animals like cattle or sheep. To be sure, some were aware that both the United States and

Russia had stockpiles of deadly anthrax spores to be used to infect enemy troops or even civilian populations if war broke out, but this seemed a remote possibility. Then some twisted terrorist—whether domestic or foreign is not yet known—began mailing anthrax-laced letters to prominent members of Congress and to national media icons like Tom Brokaw.

Overnight, anthrax became a household word. Yet, few know what the symptoms of the disease are, how it is spread, or what the danger is to the general population. The CDC reports that, "Anthrax is an acute infectious disease caused by the spore-forming bacterium Bacillus anthracis. Anthrax most commonly occurs in hoofed mammals and can also infect humans. The serious forms of human anthrax are inhalation anthrax, cutaneous anthrax, and intestinal anthrax. Initial symptoms of inhalation anthrax infection may resemble a common cold. After several days, the symptoms may progress to severe breathing problems and shock. Inhalation anthrax is often fatal."

In the case of Post Office workers who handled the infected mail sent to Congress and the media, the fatalities occurred far too often. And they had no warning, no chance to seek treatment, no avenue ahead but death. Then there was the elderly lady in Connecticut who—in a 1-in-10-million stroke of ill fate—opened a letter that had been infected in a contaminated post office. She died without ever knowing what had killed her.

What are the chances that you will receive an anthrax-infected letter? Or walk into a mall where anthrax spores have just been spread around like seeds sown across a field? The only ones who know are the terrorists who assault our society.

It is tempting to think of more well-known diseases such as malaria, cholera, typhus, meningitis, encephalitis, and tuberculosis as having been conquered by modern medicine, and no longer a threat to humankind. Tempting, but not realistic. Whether viruses, bacteria, parasites, prions, or whatever, any of the causative agents of these diseases could mutate tomorrow. It's happened innumerable times in the past, and there can be no doubt that it will happen again. What will we do the next time a pandemic strikes? We have guns and bombs to battle and kill human terrorists, but no vaccines to wage war against new armies of viral and bacterial terrorists even now preparing their invasion.

The conflict to come is between the human species and bugs too small to see. We have brains and reason and the ability to innovate on our side. Through evolution and dumb luck, we have overcome nearly all, on our journey from primitive humans to the dominant species on Earth. But our invisible enemies are a formidable force. Whereas modern humankind has only been around for the past 100 centuries, viruses, bacteria, and parasites have existed for millions of years. They witnessed the dinosaurs come and go, and all life before and after. Perhaps, to the bugs that sow death, we are merely a bump in the road.

CYBERTERRORISM

Along New Jersey's north central coast lay the receiving port for oil super-tanker shipments, a massive complex of storage tanks in a metal web of pipes, locks, valves, and refineries. One of the most important oil storage sites on the East Coast, it was largely automated, with computer guidance systems to manage the machinery, enabling a small workforce to control and direct the multiform processes of the facility.

One April weekday, a force reached into the computerized control banks and hijacked them. A series of coded commands opened some valves, closed others, speeded up the flow rate in some pipes, and throttled down the pumps in other areas. In the control room, technicians and board operators stared in disbelief as the complex's automated machinery took on a will of its own. Needles on gauges slammed into danger zones, warning lights flashed red, and buzzers and warning klaxons sounded. The operators broke into a frenzy, pushing buttons, throwing switches, cueing keyboard commands—all to no avail. Someone or something else was at the controls.

Pipelines burst from volumes and pressures far exceeding their design. Pipes ruptured at junction points resulting in optimum damage, almost as if they'd been selected to achieve that very result. Geysers of oil erupted throughout the complex, flooding it in a foul, oily black tempest. Oil storage drums emptied themselves as fast as they could, spilling thousands of gallons by the minute into the Kill van Kull, the twisting waterway accessing the complex.

Just as the complex began to self-destruct, an oil supertanker was completing the intricate series of elephantine maneuvers designed to berth it safely in a mooring slip along the docks, where it would hook itself up to the pipes and pumps designed to empty the lake of oil in its hold. Now, a gargantuan automated crane mounted on a set of railroad tracks lumbered into action, bearing down on the supertanker alongside the dock. In the crane's operating cab, the chief and two assistants tore at the controls, white-faced and cursing as the machinery refused to cooperate, obeying the commands of an unknown, unseen master.

Edging the ship, the crane released a pair of massive hooks mounted on cables—hooks big enough to hoist and handle a railroad car. The hooks plunged through the upper deck, making a horrendous clamor, shattering and battering steel support struts and internal trusses, sending off showers of sparks. Fires broke out, and it only took one of them to ignite the river of black oil flooding the docks and spilling in broad sheets into the waterway. The entire facility exploded into an inferno and a noxious pall of choking smoke began to blacken the sky as strings of exploding oil storage tanks lit it from below.

Less than a week later, the nation had barely begun to comprehend the extent of the destruction when disaster struck again. Chicago's O'Hare Airport, hub of the nation's air transport system, was experiencing a typically busy night of crowded skies and heavy air traffic when the system was turned inside out. The intrusion was subtle at first, affecting a series of number combinations. The digits were data read-outs from the different flights into, out of, or circling the airport, as seen on the computerized monitoring boards of the control tower's air-traffic controllers, the complex calculations that enabled the controllers to juggle them all safely.

Sometime around 10 P.M., the numbers started going wrong. The deviations were just small enough to avoid alerting the board operators that something was amiss. The deviations progressively added up to significant numeral factors. Those factors were expressed in the mid-air collision of two passenger planes, killing hundreds outright and wreaking havoc from the flaming debris that rained down on the inhabited landscape below.

Three days later, at Ronald Reagan Airport in Washington, D.C., the same thing happened, this time in midday, in broad daylight. A new variant had entered the picture. Some aircraft were inundated with a multiplicity of signals, effectively jamming their avionics and onboard sensors, blinding them in midair. Flaming pinwheels that were airliners plunged into the Potomac. It was later determined that the jamming frequencies had originated from a ground-based transmitter, an unknown mobile uplink unit programmed to beam the array of interference bands that jammed the aircrafts' comm links.

One thing was clear—this was enemy action. The Washington airstrike alerted investigators to probe more deeply into the Chicago disaster, leading to the discovery that it, too, had been deliberately caused. Testimony from survivors of the New Jersey oil blast broadened the scope of the menace. The United States was under attack—cyberattack.

Every computer was only a modem dial-up away. A cadre of cold-blooded, computer-hacking professionals were striking at America through the soft underbelly of its intricate technological infrastructure. Not saboteurs, but *cyberteurs*. The attackers were faceless, stateless entities in cyberspace. These were no religion-maddened would-be martyrs, seeking paradise on the wings of a suicide attack. These Internet commandos liked living. Safe in their lairs, their armaments a bank of computers, they launched their attacks from their keyboards. Knowing how to cover their tracks, they sent their signals halfway around the world to zap a target in the next town over. They might be in the United States or Europe or anywhere else. One thing was certain: Their level of professional expertise, depth of talent, and synchronized attacks indicated state backing. But which state? The United States has many enemies worldwide. The cyberattacks need not be launched from the host country. In fact, it's preferable not to, to provide an additional layer of deniability.

As a preventive measure, it had been decided some time ago to clean up radioactive waste storage sites, centralizing them to avoid providing a number of targets for potential terrorists. This involved a long-term project of shipping the waste to the new storage site in Yucca Mountain, Nevada. A load of radioactive waste was slated to be shipped from a site not far from the nuclear facility at Oak Ridge, Tennessee. The toxic radioactive slag was loaded into sealed, lead-lined containers and loaded onto flatbed railroad cars. The train was heavily guarded, with a full complement of armed troops onboard. Additional security would be provided by chase cars, which would pace the train on roads parallel to the railroad line, and by helicopters and an aerial surveillance plane. As an extra precaution, key junctions and crossings along the route would also be guarded by the local police and sheriff's department until the train had safely passed. Details of the move were supposed to be a tightly held secret, but how secret can something that big be, known to that many people?

The train went west, following a route cleared well in advance. But the line was computerized, and that was its weak link. A system of sensors interwove the miles of track, the crossings and lights and switches punctuating the cross-country route at regular intervals.

The train was still in Tennessee when an intruder signal closed one set of switches and opened another. The train was diverted onto a branch line—which brought it into a head-on collision with a freight train. The waste hauler's locomotive accordioned and the line of railroad cars jack-knifed and derailed. A string of containers were hurled into a rocky gorge where they broke open on the rocks, loosing masses of nuclear sludge and red-hot radioactive waste, poisoning the site, contaminating the water table, and turning a once-lovely stretch of forested hills and winding rivers into an atomic wasteland.

It had all been done by a nameless, faceless operator at a keyboard, one of a twilight cadre wreaking havoc on the United States. Most frightening of all was the silence. No group popped up to take credit or make demands or even taunt the great superpower. The enemy only waited in silence for a chance to strike again.

W hat shall we do when the babies start dying? A million in a single day, five million in a week. Infants pink and rosy, with smiles full of the promise of life when they're put in their cribs at night, and blue, cold, and dead in the morning.

Picture the horrible spectacle of countless tiny corpses stacked up in mortuaries like so many cords of wood. Imagine the torrents of tears as the doll-size caskets are lowered one after another into their graves.

Such unimaginable agony is but a keystroke away.

The man who coined the word *cyberterrorism*, Barry C. Collin, senior research fellow at the Institute for Security and Intelligence, wrote this sobering assessment of the cyberterrorist threat to our children in his superbly researched study, *From Virtual Darkness: New Weapons in a Timeless Battle*.

"A cyberterrorist will remotely access the processing control systems of a cereal manufacturer, change the levels of iron supplement, and sicken and kill the children of a nation enjoying their food. That cyber-terrorist will then perform similar remote alterations at a processor of infant formula."

The terrorists who hate America and Americans with an intensity forged in the fires of ignorance, jealousy, and fear know that they could strike no more terrible blow against us than to kill our children. Before the horror of September 11, 2001, most of us found it hard to fathom such evil. Surely no human—no movement—could be so possessed by the devil that they would take a baby's life with less compunction than snuffing out a candle? Then came the most terrible fall day in the history of America. More than 3,000 innocent men, women, and children were murdered in a single morning, and we came to know that men with black hearts really do dwell among us.

The insidious nature of cyberterrorism lies in our powerlessness to fight this new enemy with conventional weapons or tactics. We are not up against a hostile army armed with guns, tanks, and planes, or terrorists who attack with bombs, poison gas, or weapons of mass destruction. Rather, we are facing foes who can cripple our country's infrastructure and kill hundreds of thousands by simply punching keys on a computer keyboard.

The cyberterrorist has an added advantage: He does not have to expose himself personally to danger while carrying out his aggression. Indeed, a cyberterrorist can attack us from another continent by accessing our computer systems through the Internet.

A REAL AND GROWING THREAT

There can be no doubt that cyberterrorism poses a very real and growing threat for the United States and other technology-dependant nations. Testifying before Congress, John Deutch, director of the Central Intelligence Agency (CIA), called cyberterrorism "the ultimate precision-guided weapon." Deutch warned our nation's lawmakers that the ability to carry out such attacks is already in the hands of several terrorist organizations, including Hezbollah, the network of Middle East murderers responsible for the deaths of hundreds of Israelis.

Fred Levien, chairman of the information warfare program at the Naval Postgraduate School in Monterey, California, believes that, "There is a tremendous amount [of cyberterrorism] going on that is not let out to the public, and some of it is bordering on the catastrophic.

CHAPTER 8: CYBERTERRORISM

"Nobody wants to admit they have a system that is vulnerable to terrorism, but anybody who owns one knows there are particular areas that can be infiltrated."

In a stark warning that raised the hair on the necks of Americans who remember World War II, the President's Commission on Critical Infrastructure Protection (PCCIP) issued a report in 1998 saying, "There is an increasing threat that the US could suffer something similar to an *Electronic Pearl Harbor*." (Italics added.)

The very possibility that vital segments of our national infrastructure could be crippled by these technologically sophisticated criminals has been enough to force both government and private industry to spend billions of dollars erecting firewalls and encrypting sensitive computer files to keep cyberterrorists from either stealing critical information or shutting down systems altogether. The designing of innovative defenses against cyberterrorists has taken on new urgency recently with the revelation that more and more countries hostile to the United States—and a burgeoning number of terrorist movements—have the tools to penetrate and cripple our computerized information systems.

Collin postulates other dire threats from computer-savvy terrorists. "A cyberterrorist will place a number of computerized bombs around a city, all simultaneously transmitting unique numeric patterns, each bomb receiving each other's pattern. If bomb one stops transmitting, all the bombs detonate simultaneously.

"The keys: The cyberterrorist does not have to be strapped to any of these bombs; no large truck is required [as in the Oklahoma City bombing]; the number of bombs and urban dispersion are extensive; the encrypted patterns cannot be predicted and matched through alternate transmission [by law enforcement agencies]; the number of bombs prevents disarming them all simultaneously. *The bombs detonate*." (Italics added.)

Of course, if you live or work in an urban area that might be a likely target of terrorists—like New York, Chicago, or Los Angeles—you can always hop on a jet and fly off to the safety and tranquility of the Virgin Islands or Tahiti. But only if you're willing to take the chance that on your way to paradise you may be sipping a soda at 30,000 feet in the air one minute, and in the next, find yourself 30,000 feet beneath the sea.

"A cyberterrorist will attack the next generation of air traffic control systems and collide two large civilian aircraft," Collins goes on to predict. "This is a realistic scenario, since the cyberterrorist will also crack the aircraft's in-cockpit sensors. Much of the same can be done to the rail lines."

So public transportation is out. But you have a few bucks put aside and you've made some savvy investments. Nothing to stop you from taking your money out of the bank, selling your stock, packing the SUV, and heading for a cabin in North Dakota. Unless, of course, you can't access your savings or brokerage account. Collin issues the dark prediction that, "A cyberterrorist will disrupt the banks, the international financial transactions, the stock exchanges. The key: The people of a country will lose all confidence in the economic system."

Time for a tranquilizer. Or is it? "A cyberterrorist will remotely alter the formulas of medication at pharmaceutical manufacturers," Collins goes on. "The potential loss of life is unfathomable."

Well, at least you've still got the secure haven of your house. Or do you?

"The cyberterrorist may then decide to remotely change the pressure in the gas lines, causing a valve failure, and a block of a sleepy suburb detonates and burns. Likewise, the electrical grid is becoming steadily more vulnerable."

Just how penetrable our national electrical suppliers are was emphasized in an article in the *Dow Jones News* by Erik Baard. Baard interviewed a member of an elite computer-hacker group named "Mudge" who claimed that he could black out 30 U.S. electric utility grids. Beaard writes in his article that, "Both Mudge and the Federal Bureau of Investigation (FBI) point out that utilities are especially vulnerable because they've hired so many consultants [in late 1999] to root out their Y2K problems, essentially letting strangers poke around their most sensitive systems."

In the same article, Scott Bradner, senior technical consultant at Harvard University and vice president for standards with the Internet Society, comments, "Mudge may be right about duplicitous Y2K contract workers."

Testifying before the Senate Judiciary Subcommittee on Technology and Terrorism, Michael A. Vatis, director of the FBI's National Infrastructure Protection Center, addressed the same concern. "This is [an ongoing] problem. At any time, the grid could fall prey to rogue programmers, cyberterrorists, hostile governments, or criminal syndicates."

Is there no place safe from cyberterrorists? The short answer is no. The pervasiveness of computers, the wide-open Internet, and the ever-expanding ability of hackers to access the internal computer networks of both government agencies and private corporations has made most of the world vulnerable to computer sabotage.

> Cyberterrorists now possess the tools to shut down gas, oil, and electricity providers in the middle of winter.

Cyberterrorists now possess the programming tools to shut down gas, oil, and electricity providers in the middle of winter. Imagine living in Wisconsin or Wyoming in the bitterly cold month of March and suddenly being unable to heat your home when the temperature outside is below zero. You couldn't seek warmth in a public shelter or private business because they, too, would be without fuel. The number of people who freeze to death could mount into the millions.

Some might be able to seek warmth in a public shelter or private business for a while, but only so long as there was fuel for back-up generators. When the fuel ran out—as it inevitably would within a matter of days—those who sought refuge in a public facility would freeze to death along with the millions in private homes.

An even scarier scenario is the possibility that a cyberterrorist could penetrate the computerized controls of a nuclear power plant and deliberately cause a meltdown of the core, spreading massive amounts of radioactive material over the surrounding area. Although access to the controls of a nuclear power plant by an outside terrorist or hacker is theoretically impossible, in the emerging era of wireless computer communications this may no longer be the case.

An even more direct threat lies in the possibility that terrorists could infiltrate a nuclear power plant and gain direct control of the computer systems operating the facility.

In mock "force-on-force" exercises conducted by the Nuclear Regulatory Agency (NRA) to test security measures at nuclear power plants, the ersatz saboteurs gained access to supposedly secure areas and, in one case, even made it all the way to the plant's control room!

Consider for a moment the terrible consequences if the NRA teams had been real terrorists possessing the codes necessary to reprogram the plants' computer controls. A nuclear power plant contains over a thousand times the radiation released during an atomic blast. Should terrorists succeed in causing a meltdown of a reactor core, tens of thousands of men, women, and children living near the plant could die slow, agonizing deaths. At the same time, a vast area downwind from the reactor would become an uninhabitable nuclear wasteland, a radioactive cancer festering on the body of America.

How would terrorists gain access to heavily guarded computer codes? The answer is that these codes are not as secure as the NRA and the nuclear power industry would have the general public believe. Sensitive and supposedly safe electronic documents—including security plans stored on computer disks—have disappeared from power plants and government facilities. In May 2000, two hard drives containing top-secret nuclear information from the Los Alamos National Laboratory mysteriously vanished from a supposedly secure vault. Several weeks later, the hard drives were found in an area that had already been thoroughly searched. Unbelievably, an assistant U.S. attorney decided in January 2002 to close the case without the perpetrators being apprehended—yet one has to assume that the hard drives didn't walk out of the vault on their own.

What are U.S. officials—in particular the NRC—doing to plug the gaping holes in nuclear power plant security? According to many experts, not nearly enough. Paul Leventhal of the Nuclear Control Institute, in a commencement address to the Franklin & Marshall class of 2001, voiced this warning: "The NRC refuses to take enforcement action in response to the [security] failures, and is in the process of weakening the rules of the game in response to industry complaints."

"Sabotage of nuclear power plants may be the greatest domestic vulnerability in the United States today," he added. "This is the time to strengthen, not weaken, nuclear regulation."

A recent article on the website produced by Three Mile Island Alert, Inc. (TMIA), a nonprofit organization dedicated to improving nuclear power-plant safety, also carried a blistering assessment of the NRC. "The U.S. Nuclear Regulatory Commission has a long history of security problems. Federal oversight committees and reports by the U.S. Government Accounting Office have been extremely critical of security within the nuclear power industry.

"Because of recent events [the 9/11 attacks] and the continuing vulnerabilities that must be addressed, and because the NRC has now reduced certain security regulations, *we believe it is now necessary for public disclosure and public pressure to compel the NRC to close these security gaps.*" (Italics added.)

Although there is a very real threat that cyberterrorists will succeed in penetrating the security system of one or more of our nuclear power plants and release a shroud of radioactivity to poison our people and our land, saboteurs armed with computers and programming skills may pose an even greater menace to other critical parts of our national infrastructure.

The list of potential targets is sobering, and includes water-treatment plants, waste disposal plants, hospitals, ATM machines, electronic commerce systems, the IRS, and agency systems for Social Security, Medicare, Unemployment, and Welfare. Cyberterrorists could also shut down law-enforcement communications and records systems; airline reservations and scheduling capabilities; broadcast television, cable, and satellite transmissions; printing plants; the Internet; and e-mail.

> Not even our military is safe from sabotage by cyberterrorists.

MILITARY VULNERABILITIES

Not even our military—the most powerful fighting force the world has ever known—is safe from sabotage by cyberterrorists. In a paper titled "Cybercrime ... Cyberterrorism ... Cyberwarfare" put out by the Center for Strategic and International Studies (CSIS), Judge William H. Web-ster, Project Chair, and Arnaud de Borchgrave, Project Director, pulled no punches in their assessment of the cyberthreat. "Security is no longer defined by armed forces standing between the aggressor and the homeland. The weapons of information warfare can outflank and circumvent military establishments and compromise the underpinnings of both U.S. military and civilian infrastructure, which is now one and the same."

There are tens of thousands of cyberattacks against the Pentagon each year, and almost all are routed through other countries to camouflage their origin. As Webster and de Borchgrave point out, information-warfare specialists at the Pentagon estimate that a well-coordinated attack by a few dozen highly trained cyberterrorists *could bring the United States to its knees.*" (Italics added.)

In several recent exercises, U.S. intelligence agencies staged mock cyberattacks on sensitive government computer systems to gauge how vulnerable these systems were to cyberterrorists. The exercises revealed major flaws in our government's computer security. As an example, during one sham attack, intelligence specialists managed to shut down a large segment of the country's power grid and knock out the command and control system of the Pacific Command in Honolulu.

There can be no doubt that our enemies are only too aware of how vulnerable the computer systems of our military and our intelligence-gathering agencies really are. Michael Vatis recently told the Senate Judiciary Committee that hostile foreign nations know that they cannot defeat the United States in a conventional military confrontation and are therefore far more likely to launch cyberattacks on our vulnerable computer systems.

Yonah Alexander, director of the Center for Counter Terrorism Studies at the Potomac Institute for Policy Studies, said in 1999, "I look at the nature of the threat and I think we are actually dealing with war, a war that is going to intensify in the future. Information systems can be labeled as weapons. The war can be bloodless, but very devastating."

Today, there is not a hostile intelligence service or terrorist group in the world that doesn't know that knocking out America's critical computer systems would be far more cataclysmic to our country than inflicting a battlefield defeat on our military forces. Evidence abounds that terrorists are increasingly shifting their focus to what they perceive as our Achilles Heel: our almost total dependence on computer-automated systems to control the daily and long-term operations of our armed forces.

In a 1999 article for InfoWorld Electric, Nancy Weil, a Boston correspondent for IDG News Service, wrote of a closed Congressional hearing in which Clinton administration Deputy Defense Secretary John Hamre, who oversaw computer security for the Pentagon, met with U.S. lawmakers to discuss recent incidents of cyberterrorism.

> Knocking out America's critical computer systems would be far more cataclysmic than a battlefield defeat.

The attempted infiltration included attacks on two consecutive days in January 1999 on classified U.S. Air Force computers at Kelly Air Force Base in San Antonio. "That base operates the country's most sensitive Air Force intelligence," Weil reported, "including data relied on by troops involved in actions in Bosnia and Iraq."

Consider for a moment the worst-case scenario: Cybersaboteurs in the employ of a hostile rogue nation—North Korea, Libya, Iran, Iraq, take your pick—succeed in penetrating and shutting down the central computer systems critical to the operations of our Army, Navy, and Air Force. They also knock out the computers that control our global missile-defense network—a complex of highly sophisticated, satellite-linked observation posts that extends from the Arctic to the western Pacific to Asia. Blind to what is coming at us through the sky, we would have no chance to stop a missile attack launched against our nation—and our enemies know it!

Could it happen? We know that North Korea already has medium-range missiles capable of reaching Japan, and that they are working on intercontinental ballistic missiles (ICBMs) that could cross the Pacific and obliterate cities from Seattle to Chicago. Iraq is also known to be working on the development of medium- and long-range missiles—Israel would likely be the first target—and intelligence analysts believe that Iran may have purchased missile technology from sources in the Asian republics, such as Uzbekistan, of the former Soviet Union. If Saddam Hussein, Moammar Qadafi, or any other ruthless dictator—and there are many—were to succeed in knocking out our national-defense computer systems and launch a missile attack against the United States, we would be at their mercy.

Compounding the difficulty of guarding against cyberterrorist infiltration of our computerized military command and control structure is the fact that cyberattacks do not necessarily originate in countries that are hostile to the United States, such as Iraq, Iran, or North Korea. Penetration attempts have also come from Canada, Norway, Germany, and other allied or friendly countries. While it may turn out that most of the assaults were the work of relatively innocuous hackers who merely intended to cause mischief—in 1964, a 16-year-old English boy disabled more than 100 U.S. defense systems—it is also possible that the assaults were carried out by highly trained cybersaboteurs working for either terrorist groups or rogue nations.

How do security experts and agencies differentiate between hackers and cyberterrorists? In most cases, it's extremely complicated and difficult. Less-sophisticated hackers can now be fairly easily traced and identified. But the more adept saboteurs—whether genius hackers or well-trained cyberterrorists—are far harder to apprehend, for they know well how to cover their electronic tracks. Apprehending infiltrators can only grow more difficult as computers become more and more powerful. It is unlikely that a hacker—no matter how wealthy or intelligent—could gain access to a supercomputer such as the Cray T3D. But it is entirely possible that rogue nations could already possess these incredibly powerful processors.

A Cray T3D, for instance, can execute an incredible one trillion calculations per second. If a clever cyberterrorist were to program one or more of these supercomputers to ferret out the passwords and codes that give entry to our military computer systems, there can be little doubt that they could infiltrate many of the Pentagon's networks in a relatively short time. Once the terrorists had penetrated the security of a given system, the road would be open to send out bogus electronic instructions that could cripple not only our military but also other vital American local and national infrastructures.

If terrorists simultaneously sabotaged the computerized operations of water treatment and waste disposal plants in heavily populated areas of the eastern, midwestern, and western United States, the entire country could rapidly sink into an abyss of pandemic diseases.

CHAPTER 8: CYBERTERRORISM

American medical care is among the best in the world, and under ordinary circumstances our hospitals and private physicians could treat and cure hundreds of thousands or even millions of victims. But what if the cybersaboteurs also shut down the computer systems and communications of our nation's medical-care providers? Anyone who has been in a hospital lately knows that almost every procedure—from diagnosis to the monitoring of organs, to the use of x-ray equipment and CAT-scans, to the functions of an operating room—depend almost entirely on computers. If private physicians and clinics were unable to access their patients' computer files, doctors would find it all but impossible to effectively treat the sick, and countless Americans would likely perish.

Equally terrifying is the possibility that cyberterrorists could shut down the computer systems of the Social Security Administration and the Department of Health and Human Services, the arm of our government responsible for administering Medicare and Medicaid. If the computer systems of these agencies suddenly went down, Washington would have no way to dispense crucial Social Security checks and medical help to those segments of our society who most need government assistance—the elderly and the poor. Without the data stored in computer programs, the bureaucrats in Washington would have no way of knowing who was supposed to receive what assistance.

If the terrorists only succeeded in shutting down the government's computer systems for a day or a week, that would be bad enough. But what would happen if the cybersaboteurs were able to break into government data banks and change vital information about individuals?

Even if the agencies were able to bring their computer networks back online relatively quickly, the vast systems would be useless if the names, ages, addresses, and amounts of monthly checks had been erased or obscured. Would the bureaucracy be able to use backup drives and disaster-recovery techniques to restore computer files? Perhaps. Then again, we are not talking about simple hackers here, only able to do damage that may quickly be remedied. We are facing sophisticated cyberterrorists who would know full well about computer data backup systems, and how to cripple these as well.

It would be a human tragedy of unimaginable proportions: hundreds of thousands of elderly Americans cut off from the Social Security checks that are their only means of buying food and clothing and paying their utility bills.

The cyberterrorists could also alter personal information about Medicare and Medicaid recipients, either cutting them off from life-saving treatment entirely or tampering with their medical records and prescriptions, blinding doctors to existing conditions and causing them to unwittingly administer the wrong—perhaps lethal—medication.

Although the weak and the poor have always been the most vulnerable members of any society, in today's brave new world of technology, almost all of us have our financial, medical, and lifestyle information entered in a data bank somewhere. Personal details we would never dream of sharing with anyone but family or close friends are now accessible to faceless strangers. Our credit rating, our savings, our family history—indeed our very identity—can be stolen or altered by cyber-criminals.

Even the smartest and most financially secure among us are at risk that terrorists could access our most sensitive information and use it against us. While larcenous hackers may set out to steal the credit-card and checking-account PIN numbers of anyone regardless of income, cyberterrorists are more likely to target wealthy people with fat bank accounts and stock portfolios. As of this writing, nearly three million American households have at least $1 million in liquid assets, not including the value of their homes. Approximately 330,000 families are in the $5 million category, and another 40,000 are worth $10 million or more. All these millionaires are vulnerable to having their fortunes decimated by cyberterrorists, either through outright theft or as a result of having assets made inaccessible by changing account names, numbers, and codes.

Obviously, controls are in place that would alert banking authorities if the funds in the accounts of hundreds of thousands of very wealthy people were abruptly transferred to a single recipient. However—the question hovers—are the existing national and international banking controls sufficient to stop cybersaboteurs from plundering your bank and brokerage accounts?

The short answer is no. And so is the long answer. In recent years, cybercriminals have penetrated supposedly super-secure private and corporate bank accounts and have electronically stolen tens of millions of dollars. So far, these thefts have been relatively isolated and the victims were compensated because the amount of money stolen—although amounting to millions of dollars—was well within the range of the compensation that insurance companies expect to pay out to victims of financial fraud.

CYBERCRIME ON THE GRAND SCALE

But what would happen if the computer fraud were carried out on a massive scale by a well-organized terrorist group like al Qaeda, or the government-backed operatives of a rogue nation like Iraq? Do you have enough cash in your wallet or purse or secret stash to keep your family fed for days, weeks, or months?

If saboteurs are able to knock out U.S. computer systems on a national scale—remember, the Internet is like an octopus with tentacles reaching everywhere—the company or small business you work for will be crippled, unable to manufacture goods, provide services, or carry on other forms of commerce. Even those companies that have internal computer systems that are inaccessible to terrorists—or that can continue to operate without computers—will have to shut down because the trucking, railroad, and airline industries will all be paralyzed, and there will be no way to ship products or bring in supplies.

If a corporation is not functioning—not earning income—it will have little choice but to lay off workers. As more and more businesses close their doors, subcontractors will also be forced to fold their tents. Inevitably, unemployment will skyrocket and productivity, the economy, and society will spiral downward.

As frightening as the collapse of our economy is, the prospect that our local and national law enforcement agencies could be paralyzed by cyberterrorists is even more alarming. If police communications networks are shut down, people would have no way to call in reports of crimes. Alarm systems in banks, businesses, and private homes would also fall silent. Even if a robbery victim jumped in his or her car and sped to the local station for help, the police would be unable to dispatch their officers in the field to the crime scene. A car could be a block from where a vicious murder was being committed, and the officers would have no idea. Even if a felon were apprehended in the midst of his or her misdeed, without access to fingerprint and criminal history records, the police would have no idea whether the individual they had in custody was a relatively harmless petty crook or a wanted mass murderer.

On a national scale, without access to federal and state criminal data banks, it is doubtful that the FBI could effectively pursue the serial killers, rapists, kidnappers—and now terrorists—that represent the gravest threat to our lives, property, and peace of mind. The crime-solving resources of the FBI—their investigative techniques, forensic laboratories, fingerprint records, files on criminals and terrorists, and dozens of other known and covert means of bringing in the bad folks—make the FBI a most formidable force in the battle against both domestic crime and international terrorism.

Yet the FBI and all other U.S. law enforcement and intelligence agencies have a fallibility—an almost total reliance on the gathering and dissemination of information through computers. If cyberterrorists should succeed in disabling the cyberlinks between our federal, state, and local police forces, calamity awaits in the wings. National and local law enforcement would regress to the primitive, pre-computer level of the 1930s. In that era, the only way to get the fingerprints, photos, and records of criminals from one place to another was by courier or mail.

While domestic law enforcement would be severely hampered if the police and the FBI lost the use of their computer and communications systems, cyberterrorists could do even more damage to our foreign intelligence gathering capability. The CIA, National Security Agency, and other government intelligence-gathering organizations simply cannot function without computers. The mass of intelligence information that comes in every day from spy satellites, electronic intercepts, surveillance ships, and U.S. and allied operatives is so massive in volume and scope that only computers can coordinate and analyze the data.

Today, television also plays a vital role in bringing criminals to justice. Perhaps the most effective TV crime-fighting tool is the show

America's Most Wanted, which provides photographs of felons and accounts of their crimes. To date, the show has led directly to the capture of several hundred dangerous fugitives. Television news shows—especially local broadcasts—also play a vital role in the battle against crime by airing the pictures and profiles of felons in prime time when millions are watching. Quite often someone in the viewing audience will leap up from the couch, shout, "Damn, I know that person," and call the police. It happens every day in some part of the country. Of course, if cyberterrorists are able to knock out the computers and satellites that control television broadcasting, the consequences will go far beyond hamstringing the nation's capacity to fight crime. Hundreds of millions of people—both in the United States and around the world—depend on TV to provide not only entertainment but also news, weather, and other information that helps people make decisions about their daily lives.

Television also influences the manner in which governments form national and international policy. Were we to be suddenly deprived of the vast store of information that television disseminates to millions each day, both private individuals and governments might make misjudgments that could lead to social chaos, a heightening of existing hostilities, or even war.

Consider this all-too-plausible scenario. As this book is being written, India and Pakistan are perhaps one step away from going to war over the disputed province of Kashmir. These two countries are separated not just by a border but by religious fanaticism. The population of India is predominately Hindu, while the Pakistanis are overwhelmingly Muslim. So far, the collective tempers of these two volatile peoples have been kept in check, largely through calming news broadcasts by their own governments and the international media. But suppose those broadcasts suddenly ceased. It is not hard to imagine the inflammatory rumors that would soon run rife, and the war fever and panic that would inevitably follow. How long could war be avoided if Pakistani terrorists once again began murdering Indian government officials and hijacking Indian planes, and Indian mobs sacked and burned the Pakistani embassy, massacring the Muslim diplomats inside?

What is truly terrifying is that both countries possess nuclear weapons and the missiles to deliver them. If cyberterrorists should suddenly black out the broadcast media in India and Pakistan—and successfully cripple other forms of computer and satellite-based communications in this explosive region of the world—the terrible result could be the first use of nuclear weapons since the United States dropped atomic bombs on Hiroshima and Nagasaki at the end of World War II.

Whether thinking about the lives of our young, about our personal safety, or about the security of our country, we are in the headlights of cyberterrorists like a startled deer on a moonless night. The United States possesses the most powerful military machine in the history of humankind, and a vibrant economy that yields wealth for all Americans—indeed for half the world—on a scale unimagined before our nation came to be.

Yet as powerful as we are, we can be brought to our knees, not by an army of people and murderous machines, but by a simple assault of 1 and 0 digits. Will we—as a people and a nation—survive a computer attack on the critically and shamefully vulnerable infrastructures that glue us all together?

Tune in tomorrow.

INSECT INVASIONS

In a vast landscape of Nebraska farmlands, a vista of gently rounded hills and endless golden wheat fields, something was wrong. The scene thrummed with an eerie, echoing reverberation, an almost mechanical whirring that shivered both heaven and Earth.

It was several weeks short of harvest time. The wheat yield promised to be a good one, one of the best in the last decade. Times were always hard for farmers, but the recent years of wild weather and other climatic changes brought about by global warming had made farming a nightmarish ordeal—not only in Nebraska, but throughout the United States and Canada, as well as overseas. This year's harvest, however, promised to be a record breaker. There'd been plenty of rain and sunshine at all the right times, and now thousands of square miles of prime wheat fields flourished full and golden under a clear, cloudless sky.

All should have been well, but there was a threat of invaders. Humanity's claim to dominion over all living things on Earth was no longer unchallenged. The new claimants for the title of overlords of the planet had sent representatives to the Nebraska wheat fields, to contend with the farmers for the fruit of their backbreaking, endless dusk-to-dawn laboring, chores, and drudgery.

The enemy was airborne. That unearthly, keening drone was the sound of their oncoming air force, closing in on the endless acres of golden wheat. The farmers were out in force, in the fields, looking up—waiting for the enemy to show themselves.

So they did, appearing as a cloud on the southeastern horizon. The cloud grew, widening and darkening, expanding to enfold the sky in a humming, buzzing, seething pall. The droning grew louder, vibrations rattling the skulls of the farmers huddled in small, helpless knots in their fields. They could no more resist this onslaught than they could the whirlwind. The horde of locusts closed on the beckoning wheat fields.

It used to be that Nebraska was free from locust infestations, but, like a lot of things that "used to be," such as normal weather with regular seasons that a farmer could depend on, it just wasn't that way anymore. Humanity and nature had wrought massive change: humanity, whose industrial processes had unintentionally raised the global temperature, and nature, by the way it responded to the human-made changes in the biosphere.

CHAPTER 9: INSECT INVASIONS

The immediate winner of the burgeoning world order was the bugs. In numbers and variety, the lowly insect could lay claim to the title of Earth's most successful life form. There were more than 300,000 different species of beetles alone. Insects had adapted to fill every environmental niche, on land and sea, in desert and jungle. As global warming caused vast belts of the United States to lurch from temperate to sub-tropical climes, the bugs thrived. Powering their success was their incredible reproductive fecundity, enabling them to go through a generation in a few weeks.

No less formidable was their adaptability. Humans warred endlessly with them, spraying grubs, parasitic mites, weevils, beetles, gnawers, burrowers, and a host of other crop-destroying crawlers. Bug hordes were drenched with clouds of toxic insecticides.

At first, the insecticides worked, exterminating almost all of the bugs. But never all. There were always a few survivors who, for one reason or another, perhaps something extra in their genetic makeup, could not be killed by the latest super-toxin. Inevitably they would reproduce, and their numerous progeny possessed the gene that kept a particular insecticide from killing them. Humans could not have created a breed of invincible super-bugs more effectively if they had set out to do so. New generations of bugs actually thrived on the toxins, but the rivers of insecticides pouring into the land and watercourses eventually began poisoning the farmers and their families.

Insects had turned the American South into a sinkhole of sickness. Flourishing in swamps and stagnant bodies of water, clouds of mosquitoes spread epidemics of West Nile Virus and Dengue fever to livestock and humans alike. West Nile Virus had rendered large sections of the Louisiana bayou country, the Florida Everglades, and the Galveston-Houston axis uninhabitable. Malaria had become a critical public health problem, even reaching north beyond the Mason-Dixon line to afflict the central and mid-Atlantic states.

The cities were not immune. Indigenous species of roaches and flies, thriving in the hot, damp climate, were forced to contend with their tropical cousins who'd followed the heat, migrating northward.

Throughout all but the northernmost states, colonies of fire ants took root, holding fast, multiplying, and then expanding their domain, thriving equally in town and country. Their attraction to ground-based electric cables and tendency to nest around them led to grotesque scenes of horror when unsuspecting electrical, phone, or cable technicians blundered into fire-ant nests and were stung to death by swarming hordes. More generally, pets, small children, the elderly, and the merely unwary or unlucky were liable to fall victim to the searing, agonizing bites of fire-ant mandibles.

Now came the locusts, targeting the Nebraska wheat fields. Dark, humming clouds of segmented, armored, six-legged eating machines descended, blanketing the fields, covering the rolling acres. When they finally retreated, every single stalk of wheat had been picked clean of its sun-ripened grain, leaving nothing but plucked, shredded husks and straws littering the now-bare brown ground.

It was only one of thousands of similar encounters taking place daily on the planet. The insects didn't know that they were fighting a war. No conscious decision, no strategizing directed their onslaughts against humans. They simply lived, and fed, and bred. If they caused famine among the humans, or spread virulent pandemics, it was beyond the ken of pin-sized insectoid brains.

But given the success of their increasing incursions against humanity, they might as well have been fighting a war, for the result was the same.

The bugs were winning.

The bugs are coming. Big, bad, and ravenous. Marching toward us from the tropics in legions, terrible in their appetites and terrible in their teeth. They're coming to devour everything edible in our world, and there's not a thing we can do about it. As the greenhouse effect continues to warm the world—making summers longer and winters milder—immense swarms of tropical insects are moving north into the temperate regions of the world. Malaria-carrying mosquitoes, crop-devouring desert locusts, carnivorous Army ants, and a host of other flying, crawling, hopping, inching vermin are invading regions of the earth where they have been unknown for millions of years.

KILLER BEES!

Africanized honey bees—better known as "killer bees"—are one example. This highly dangerous new species first appeared in 1956 when African bees—imported into South America by Brazilian scientists attempting to create a superior honey-producing bee—escaped into the wild and interbred with native bees. The hybrid insect that resulted from the interbreeding possessed the worst qualities of both species.

While domestic bees have bred for centuries and are long accustomed to the presence of humans and other animals, killer bees are truly wild creatures that do not easily tolerate the presence of other species. Although the murderous insects look just like domestic honey bees, they are far more aggressive. If a mammal, reptile, bird, or other insect is unwary enough to disturb one of their hives, the killer bees will pursue the victim for as far as a quarter of a mile, and sting in much greater numbers.

Since the first contact between killer bees and humans in the late 1950s, the super-aggressive insects have killed more than 1,000 people in South America, Central America, and Mexico. They have also stung tens of thousands of animals to death, including large mammals such as cows and horses.

Entomologists—scientists who study insects—knew early on that the bees would migrate steadily north through Central America and Mexico and eventually reach the United States. Yet the scientists believed that winter cold would confine the swarms to southern states such as Texas, Alabama, and Florida—and that most of the United States would escape invasion by the deadly insects. Today, however, an increasing number of entomologists believe that the bioengineered bugs could eventually spread as far north as Montana. The reasons are twofold: the warming climate due to the greenhouse effect, and the apparent ability of the Africanized bee to adapt to colder climates.

People living in suburban and rural areas face the greatest risk from the bees because of the abundance of nesting sites found in and around homes. They prefer to build their hives in tree hollows, cracks in walls, drainage pipes, sheds, bird houses, woodpiles, and under mobile homes. Because killer bees are far less discriminating than domestic bees about where they build their nests, they present a greater danger to humans. Although the insects usually establish colonies in the country, they have also been known to move into urban areas. One of the most unlikely areas that the Africanized bees have settled is the Las Vegas Strip, that mecca of flashing neon, garish hotels, and slot machines that is the playground of millions of pleasure seekers each year.

Gina Stoneking, bee coordinator for the Nevada Division of Agriculture, said in an interview with *Las Vegas Sun* reporter Mary Manning that, "At least 25 nests of the Africanized bees have been cleared away from Strip resorts in the past year. And that's only what we know about, because the pesticide companies turn them in to us, but not all of them."

In the same story, Nevada Agriculture Administrator Paul Iverson made this startling observation: "[Killer] bees will eventually determine that the Strip is a prime vacation area. As our population continues to grow, those bees will continue to come. There's no way to get rid of this bee species once it's established. We have to learn to live with them, and we will because they are here to stay."

If the mutant insects continue to multiply out of control—establishing hives in ever more heavily trafficked places like hotel entrances and parking garages—there will be no way for humans to avoid disturbing the highly territorial bees. The Africanized bees present an especially acute danger in an environment like the Las Vegas Strip because they perceive loud noises, dark clothing, shiny jewelry, and strong fragrances as threats, and are likely to attack when any of these stimuli are present. The Strip has all the elements—blaring music and clanging slot machines, men and women wearing dark clothes and ostentatious jewelry and reeking of aftershave and perfume—that are likely to make the bees aggressive. The inevitable result of a killer bee infestation would be that hundreds of people would be attacked by the vicious insects, and there will undoubtedly be fatalities. As word spreads across the country that swarms of killer bees are infesting the Strip, the tourist industry would shut down overnight, and Las Vegas would become a glittering ghost town.

How scary is the threat? In the *Sun* article, American Pest Control General Manager George Botta—who has done 400 nest removals wearing a suit like an astronaut's—was quoted as saying, "It's like a sci-fi movie out there sometimes."

The lethal insects have also infested other areas of Las Vegas, including McCarran International Airport, where they've been reported to have settled on jetliners, flown into engines and swarmed across the tarmac. Consider for a moment the implications of a swarm of killer bees flying into a jet engine as a plane is taking off. Over the years, a score of both civilian and military jets have crashed after birds flew into their engines and the planes lost power. Undoubtedly, if thousands of large bees were sucked into a jet's engines, the effect would be equally fatal.

While Las Vegas is unique in just about every way a city can be, the disaster that would follow a killer bee infestation also looms over virtually every other part of our country. The United States has an abundance of the food, water, and sugar supplies that the insects need to flourish, and this may cause a sudden huge increase in the number, size, and range of swarms.

There is also the possibility that the bioengineered bees will mutate again—not by the hand of human beings this time but by a sudden evolutionary change—and take an even more formidable form. At present, the Africanized queen bees lay an average of 1,500 eggs per day. If the egg-laying capacity of the queens doubled or tripled, within three weeks—the time it takes for a worker bee to fully develop from an egg—there would be three times as many of the murderous insects among us. The implications of an explosion of the killer bee population here are simply staggering. Thousands of people could be stung to death each year, along with hundreds of thousands of both domestic and wild animals. Heavily infested areas—including small towns, farms, and suburban tracts—would become uninhabitable. Shopping malls, factories, sports stadiums, and wilderness areas would become too dangerous to enter.

Is this scenario farfetched? Hardly. In a relatively short time, the Africanized bees have grown from a single swarm containing hundreds of insects into tens of thousands of swarms teeming with untold millions of the winged mutants. They have also flourished on three separate continents, and migrated thousands of miles north across land and sea in a matter of decades. Like most insects, Africanized bees are remarkably adaptable and opportunistic. They have learned to eat new foods, inhabit new environments, adjust to hostile climatic conditions, and rebound from human assaults with insecticides, traps, and fire. The question is not whether the killer bees will survive in our world, but whether we will survive in theirs.

> The question is not whether the killer bees will survive in our world, but whether we will survive in theirs.

LIKE ANTS AT A PICNIC

Mutant bees are not the only insect predator to reach our shores from the jungles of Central and South America; we have also been invaded by several species of ants. Not the pencil lines of tiny household pests you can dispatch with a can of Black Flag, but countless colonies with a million or more ants in each colony.

There are approximately 20,000 species of ants in the world, but the two types that pose the greatest threat to humans are army ants and fire ants. The former is a ferocious carnivore, and swarms of the beasts have been known to attack and devour humans. The latter has a poisonous bite that can set your flesh aflame.

The most dangerous ant species is the army ant. An article on the planet-pets.com website contains this horrifying description of the insects. "Army ants are specialists in carnage. They can be found in tropical forests all over the world. Traveling in groups of 10,000 to 100,000, they are the lords of the insect world, blind, carnivorous and kill every animal that remains in their path."

Army ants are truly the scourge of the jungle. Their jaws are so well adapted to slicing through flesh that they have been known to turn trapped horses into skeletons in a matter of hours."

Consider this scenario. It is the year 2012. The earth's climate has warmed enough that army ants have been able to establish colonies in the southern United States. Army ants can adapt to climate change, so the temperature won't have to rise that much. You and your family live in Mobile. It is summer. One night you go to sleep without fully closing the screen door to the patio. When you open your bedroom door the next morning, you see a trail of army ants retreating across the patio. The door to the bedroom where your child—or an invalid parent—sleeps is open. You look inside, and scream—scream until there is no breath left in your lungs—at the sight of the gleaming skull and picked-clean bones lying on the bed.

The stuff of a Steven King novel? Or future reality? Read on and decide for yourself.

To understand the threat that army ants pose to the inhabitants of the United States, Europe, and the temperate regions of Asia, we must first understand what they look like, how they live, and how they hunt. The ants have some incredible—and so far unexplained—capabilities that make them formidable. The body of an army ant has a head, thorax, and abdomen. The head has a mouth, primitive eyes, and antennae. The mouth also has two jaws called mandibles that are like scissors. Because the ants are carnivorous and live in huge colonies, they must migrate every 20 days to find fresh food. According to an article on the Insecta Inspecta World website, "Army ants kill and eat up to 100,000 animals (mostly other insects) a day. Together they can kill lizards, snakes, chickens, pigs, goats, scorpions, and many other animals. They also climb trees and eat birds, plus insects that may live in trees."

Army ants construct nests that are unique in the animal world. Their nests—called bivouacs—are made up of the ants themselves. They form a living mass by hooking onto each other using their jaws and claws. Just as in a traditional insect nest, the queen and her brood are protected by the "nest" of ant bodies around her, and food is brought inside. A colony of army ants may number over a million insects—there have been reports of colonies containing as many as 30 million ants—and consists of a single queen, her young brood, male soldiers, and female workers. The queen lays eggs, the soldiers defend the colony, and the workers forage for food, feed the queen and the soldiers, and tend the queen's brood.

The queen is the largest ant, usually twice the size of the soldiers and workers. She is the "brain" of the colony. She controls all the other ants, and the soldiers and workers are extremely protective of her. The queen's role in the colony is to produce young, and most of the time she barely moves from one location. The workers are sterile females. They are essentially blind and follow chemical trails to find their way around. They are primarily handmaidens to the queen, nannies, and waitresses serving food to the soldiers.

An article on the Army Ant web page by Zach Fulton describes the soldiers this way. "The soldiers are one to two inches long, including their two mighty mandibles. The soldiers' main jobs are to protect the queen, gather or kill food, and attack enemy colonies."

The soldiers are all males and are easily recognized by their two huge mandibles, or jaws. The soldiers use their mandibles mainly for killing prey and digging in the relatively soft earth of the rain forest. The mandibles are so immense that the soldiers cannot feed themselves and have to depend on the smaller workers to put food into their mouths.

Ron Kalasinskas writes in his fascinating book, *Animals of the Rainforest*, that, "The 'clamping power' of the jaws of an army ant is so strong that natives to the rainforest used the ants to stitch up wounds. They would place an ant over an open wound and squeeze the ant from behind so it would bite down on the wound. They would then cut off the back part of the ant's body so that the head remained clamped on the wound. By doing this with a couple of ants you have what we call 'stitches'."

If the clamping power of the mandibles of a single army ant is this great, imagine falling asleep at a picnic and waking up to find 25 or 50 of the beasts with their jaws embedded in your flesh. How could you get them off you before thousands more ants arrived and you were slowly eaten alive? Surely a nightmare that could never come true, right? Wrong. More than one entomologist has described how millions of army ants will form into an almost solid mass and march through the rain forest killing and eating both insects and animals.

The lives of army ants are divided into two distinct periods that alternate every few weeks. The first is the 20-day stationary phase during which the colony remains in one place so that the queen can lay her eggs—up to 300,000 within a few days—and the eggs can mature into adults. The second period is the 15-day migratory phase when the ants are constantly on the move in search of new feeding grounds. How do the army ants know when it is time to migrate and time to remain in one place so a new brood can be raised? Good question, and one that has not yet been answered.

Another mystery is how the essentially blind ants find their way through the dense, dark, rainforest. Dr. Nigel R. Franks, a British Professor of Animal Behavior and Ecology, believes the explanation may be that the ants are using polarized sunlight to navigate. Yet army ants have just a single facet in each eye, rather than multi-faceted compound eyes like most insects. Franks has come up with a fascinating theory. "The mystery is how the colony can navigate with each of its workers having such rudimentary eyesight," he writes in an article published in *American Scientist* titled "Army Ants: A Collective Intelligence." "In my wildest dreams, I imagine that the whole swarm behaves like a huge compound eye, with each of the ants in the swarm front contributing two lenses to a 1- or 20-m wide 'eye' with hundreds of thousands of facets."

Commenting on Franks's work in a story in Science Frontiers Online, scientist and author William R. Corliss wrote, "A colony of a million army ants is a sophisticated 'super-organism.' The colony carries out its legendary raids and can even keep nest temperatures constant to within a degree. An army ant colony seems endowed with an intelligence far beyond that of any individual ant."

If a colony of army ants is indeed a super-organism—with a million or more ants able to see and act as one—the implications for humanity could be terrifying indeed. It means that as the earth warms and the ants inevitably migrate from the tropics to the United States, Europe, and the temperate regions of Asia, we shall be faced not with ordinary ants one can squash underfoot but with a single entity having the collective

> As the earth warms and the ants inevitably migrate from the tropics, we shall be faced not with ordinary ants one can squash underfoot but with a single entity having the collective intelligence of millions.

intelligence of millions of animals. Could it be that this super-organism will be resourceful enough to do battle with humans on equal terms? When the army ants inevitably arrive, will they be able to mount a defense that thwarts everything we throw against them, and an offense that will overrun human habitats? Will they eat our chickens and cows and dogs and cats—and then us? The answer will come—perhaps not for 10 or 20 years—but it will come.

While army ants are a future threat, murderous fire ants are already among us, as a news story filed by CNN from Rancho Santa Margarita, California, confirms in gory detail: "A potentially deadly invasion is underway in Southern California. Millions of fire ants have marched to within feet of posh neighborhoods—carrying the capacity to kill. 'I think there's probably 50 to 60 people, documented cases, where fire ants killed,' said David Williams of the U.S. Agriculture Department."

Children and the elderly are the most vulnerable to fire-ant stings, the most likely to go into shock and perhaps even die if stung by a large number of the aggressive insects at once. "I've heard horrible stories about children who stood on ant hills and no one was watching ... but I'm always watching my children," said one California mother.

A single fire-ant mound can be home to as many as 200,000 ants. Like killer bees, if the ants feel threatened, they swarm out of the mound and start stinging, whether the intruder is insect, animal, or human.

Imagine for a moment that you suddenly found yourself in the midst of the nightmarish scene described by the California mother. You and your family have just set up camp for the weekend at the edge of a flowered meadow. The sky is clear, the wind is soft, and the birds are singing in the gently swaying trees above your tent. As you prepare to cook dinner, your three children are playing in the meadow.

Then your 10-year-old son emits an ear-piercing scream. "Mom, Dad, come quick!"

Your heart pounds as you race toward the open area. Your son and eight-year-old daughter are screaming and pointing at the ground. Where's your four-year-old boy?

You reach your son and daughter and gasp at the sight before you. Your youngest child is lying prone across a two-foot-high fire-ant mound, his left foot snared in a vine. He is half-covered with ants and gasping for breath.

You free your boy's foot, pull him off the mound and begin flailing at the ants with your shirt. The insects on his clothes come away, but hundreds of others have sunk their barbed mandibles into the flesh of his arms, bare legs, and face, and you kneel and start yanking them out one by one.

You're no doctor, but you know he's going into toxic shock. And the nearest hospital is at least 20 miles away. You pull away the last of the ants, pick up your son, and run for the car. Just before you reach your campsite, your feel your boy go limp. You lay him out on the picnic table and start mouth-to-mouth resuscitation. You blow air into his lungs for a minute, two minutes, five minutes, ten minutes. His chest remains still, and now he's changing color. You put him across the back seat of the car and you and the family race for the hospital.

In the emergency room, the attending physician approaches you in the waiting room with a grim face.

"I'm sorry," the doctor says. "Your boy was dead on arrival. There was nothing we could do."

Fire ants flourish in the United States because they have no natural enemies here. The insects now infest more than 300 million acres in at least 12 states, including Alabama, Arkansas, California, Florida, Georgia, Louisiana, Mississippi, North Carolina, Oklahoma, South Carolina, Tennessee, and Texas. They are expanding their range at the rate of three miles per year, and often leapfrog to new areas by hitching rides in the sod of nursery plants.

An article on the greensmiths.com web page reports that, "Fire ants expand naturally and steadily into new territory because of their high reproductive rate. Mild winter weather [in other words, the greenhouse effect] has accelerated their movement. *Current technology and efforts are not expected to reverse this growth trend in the foreseeable future."* (Italics added.)

If you are stung by fire ants, you can expect to suffer through several days of discomfort which may, in some, become severe. Within 24 hours after you have been stung, a pustule-like sore will break out at each sting site. The sting will itch incessantly, and if you scratch the wound you may cause it to rupture. This, in turn, will expose you to a secondary infection and scarring.

In his book *The Best Control, Second Edition,* author Steve Tvedten provides this vivid account of an attack by fire ants: "They can and quickly do latch onto your flesh repeatedly, pivoting in tiny circles until the victim can repel them or dies. The venom burns like a hot match and causes tiny blisters that persist for days if left untreated or for weeks if scratched or infected."

Compared to army ants, fire ants are tiny. The workers are a quarter inch long while the winged males, females, and queen are about a third of an inch in length. The ants are native to Brazil. It is believed that they reached the United States aboard a South American freighter that docked in Mobile, Alabama, in the 1930s.

They live in large, above-ground mounds that are up to 24 inches in diameter and 18 inches high. The nests may extend as much as six feet underground, and they're most often constructed in open areas such as fields, lawns, and the grassy fringes of highways. In populated areas, the insects sometimes build soil tubes on building foundations. Whether mounds or soil tubes, fire-ant nests are rarely situated in forests or other shaded areas. The mounds—and the underground chambers beneath—enable the fire ants to maintain a microclimate that is often quite different than the climate outside. By raising the temperature inside the mound, the insects are able to continue to breed through cold weather, and move into more northerly regions.

Fire ants feed on a wide spectrum of vegetation. They are a particular scourge to farmers because the ravenous insects have a special fondness for wheat, corn, and sorghum seed. They have even been known to eat dry cotton.

They are also drawn to the living flesh of warm-blooded species, especially to newborns and the very young. A story in the *St. Petersburg Times* by reporter Craig Pittman described the terrible toll fire ants have taken on wildlife in the Florida Keys. "When the fire ants encounter the young of an endangered or threatened species—everything from Schaus swallowtail butterflies to sea turtles and even Key deer—they swarm over it, stinging, blinding, and killing it."

Pittman's chilling words are given credence by a nightmarish discovery made by Eckerd College Professor Elizabeth Forys, who was part of a three-year study of endangered Lower Key marsh rabbits in the early 1990s. During her field work, Forys noticed that quite often when she when she examined a mother rabbit's den she found no babies inside, just fire ants swarming around the mouth of the burrow.

"There was no way for them to run away when they had just been born," she said."

Forys also described how the vicious fire ants attacked sea turtle eggs. "The ants did not get into the shell," she said. "What they did was make foraging trails to the eggs and check them periodically. Then on the day the turtle hatchlings began to break through the eggs, the fire ants came over en masse to attack. In half of the turtle deaths, they were never even able to leave their shells. They were killed in their eggs."

According to an article carried by the Environment News Network, entomologists are attempting to eliminate the fire ant using the pathogen *T. solenopsae*. "The pathogen ... infects ant colonies and chronically weakens them. Workers transmit the pathogen to the queen through food exchange. The disease slowly reduces the queen's weight. She lays fewer and fewer eggs, all infected with the pathogen, further weakening the colony."

While laudable, the efforts of entomologists to eliminate fire ants is akin to someone trying to empty the ocean with a bucket. There are simply too many fire-ant colonies and too few eradication programs. As the insects continue to spread into populated areas, people will be stung not just outdoors but indoors as well. In the southern states, the aggressive ants can now be found not only in private homes but in office buildings, bus and train stations, and even hospitals. Eradicating the ants indoors is more difficult because of the danger to human health posed by chemical insecticides.

Could the handwriting on the wall be any bolder? The fire ant population is exploding, and the venomous insects are inexorably spreading over more and more of the country. They're headed for our homes and workplaces, the schools where our kids learn, and the nursing homes where our elderly parents live.

And—in the absence of effective tools and technologies to fight them—all we can do is stand back and wring our hands.

DEATH, HERE IS THY STING

While the ants are crawling inexorably north across the ground, mosquitoes are increasingly clogging the air. Mosquitoes are relatively small insects usually no larger than a half-inch long. They have slender bodies, a single pair of narrow wings, and three pairs of long legs. They also have a piercing proboscis—a long beak—which the females use to suck blood from their victims.

When one studies the lifestyle of mosquitoes, the phrase "femme fatale" springs to mind. Where male mosquitoes are—in the grand scheme of nature—little more than courtesans, lucky one day, unlucky the next, female mosquitoes are busy changing the world. Ever since the Mesozoic era 245 million years ago, female mosquitoes have been voracious bloodsuckers. In the movie *Jurassic Park*, scientists extracted the blood of a dinosaur from the gut of a prehistoric mosquito. In the story, the mosquito had bitten the dinosaur and shortly afterwards had gotten itself trapped in tree sap, which, over time, became solid amber. The scientists inserted a needle through the amber into the mosquito's "stomach" and withdrew DNA from the dinosaur blood inside the insect. Is such a scenario realistic? Some researchers say yes, others say no. How is the scenario presented in *Jurassic Park* relevant to the dangers that mosquitoes pose to humanity today? Let us suppose for a moment that, sometime in the future, scientists extract the blood of an extinct animal—be it a dinosaur, saber-toothed tiger, wooly mammoth, or some other ancient beast—and the blood was infected with a long-dormant disease for which we have no defenses and no cure. Once the disease escaped from the laboratory, we would have no way to control it. If the research center is in or near a large population center, tens of thousands could be infected and die from the prehistoric killer.

It's a common misconception that mosquitoes suck blood from their victims as a form of sustenance. In fact, female mosquitoes suck the blood of their hosts not to feed themselves but to obtain protein to nourish their eggs. Most of us consider mosquitoes as merely pests that appear each summer and play havoc with barbecuing on the back lawn. In reality, a single mosquito is as dangerous to a human as a rabid pit bull. Why? Because a mosquito is a vector, a middle agent between an infected animal and an uninfected animal. In other words, a mosquito will suck the blood of a diseased mammal, reptile, or bird, and then fly on and sink its proboscis into a healthy animal—like a human—and transfer the infection. It's happened time and again throughout history, and it will happen again in the future.

If you are convinced that mosquitoes single you out to feast on, you may be right. According to a story on the Environmental News Network, mosquitoes have a greater affinity for some people than they do for others. "In a study to determine whether the tiny vampires choose their victims indiscriminately, University of Florida entomologist Jerry Butler and research assistant Karen McKenzie found that mosquitoes do, indeed, choose.

"'Undoubtedly, mosquitoes have preferences,' Butler said. 'People do differ, and in a group of 10, one person will be fed on more than others. People who think they attract mosquitoes are the ones at largest risk of mosquito-borne disease. They'll have a hundred mosquitoes feed on them when a normally repellent person might have five. It's that kind of ratio.'

"Mosquitoes have evolved and survived—even thrived, Butler points out—because of their ability to choose the best hosts for the blood meals …. They find their hosts, initially, through a keen sense of smell. People can attract mosquitoes from 40 miles away simply by breathing. When a person exhales, their carbon dioxide and other odors mix to produce a plume that travels through the air. The plume acts like a dinner bell to mosquitoes, letting them know a juicy meal is within range."

While only one mosquito in a thousand carries disease organisms, the viruses they transmit include such deadly killers as malaria, St. Louis encephalitis, Japanese encephalitis, West Nile virus, Dengue fever, yellow fever, eastern equine disease, and dog-heartworm.

Malaria is an ancient virus and one of the most widespread diseases afflicting humans. According to the World Health Organization (WHO), each year malaria infects at least 400 million people. In Africa alone, more than 2,000,000 people a year die from the disease. Once on the decline, malaria is now undergoing a resurgence, infecting more people each year and spreading into areas where it was previously unknown. The reason that the malaria threat is becoming ever more daunting is that mosquito populations—the vectors that transmit the disease—are exploding, as mean temperatures around the world continue to rise.

An article on the Global Change website put the growing problem in prospective. "What might happen if (our) climate rapidly warms as greenhouse gases accumulate in the atmosphere? Could malaria and other diseases spread over much wider areas and up to higher altitudes? Yes, say several recent studies."

A May 1995 article in *Environmental Health Perspectives* titled "Potential Impact of Global Climate on Malaria" reported the conclusion of British and Dutch scientists that the earth's warming climate may well result in a "widespread increase in risk [of disease] due to expansion of the areas suitable for malaria transmission."

Another study reported in *New Scientist* magazine in May 1995 described the climate/malaria link research done by scientists Philippe Martin and Myriam Lefebvre of the Tropical Vegetation Monitoring Unit of the European Commission's Joint Research Center. The two researchers found that the warming climate would make conditions in several regions of the world—including North America—far more favorable to the transmission of malaria by mosquitoes. They also warned that the spread of the disease to areas where people have little or no immunity could result in a malaria epidemic, and a heavy death toll.

The mosquito menace is especially acute because the insects can reproduce so rapidly. Deposited in standing water, mosquito eggs hatch in just three to five days. Although it usually takes two weeks for a new generation to reach maturity, during warm weather it is not uncommon for mosquitoes to go from pupae to the flying adult stage in as little as seven days.

Although most mosquito species overwinter in the egg stage, a few species spend the winter as adult, mated females. They usually seek out dark, protected places like cellars, sewers, and wells. When spring arrives, the insects once more become active, with both sexes feeding on nectar and the females sucking blood from mammals to nourish their eggs.

Although malaria is the most widespread mosquito-borne disease, the insects also transmit Dengue hemorrhagic fever. Symptoms include bleeding from the nose, mouth, and gums; an unquenchable thirst; and often severe difficulty in breathing.

"Dengue has been causing fever, chills and skeletal pain for many years," reads an article on the Mosquito bytes website. "After World War II, a more serious form of the disease—Dengue hemorrhagic fever—emerged in Southeast Asia, where it became one of the leading causes [of] morbidity and mortality in children."

In addition to outbreaks in Southeast Asia, Dengue hemorrhagic fever has now become established in both South and Central America, and has spread north all the way to the Texas border with Mexico. Why is the disease spreading like wildfire? There are four main reasons. The unprecedented population growth in the Third World in recent decades has resulted in sprawling slums where unsanitary living conditions allow mosquitoes to breed close to people. Secondly, the huge increase of untreated human garbage—in particular plastic packaging and dis-carded tires—has provided mosquitoes with ideal habitats. Third, mod-ern transportation—especially air travel—has allowed people infected with the disease to move from one populated area to another before the first symptoms appear. A victim may become infected in South America and be in Florida, infecting others, before the disease manifests itself. Finally, mosquito-control methods in recent years have proven ineffective in keeping down populations of disease-carrying mosquitoes.

West Nile virus (WNV) is yet another disease transmitted through the bite of infected female mosquitoes. The virus first appeared in

1937 in the West Nile District of Uganda in Africa. Since then, there have been outbreaks of the disease in Israel, France, South Africa, and, in this country, New York City. The virus has now been documented in 27 states and Washington, D.C.

Symptoms of the disease include high fever, disorientation, muscle weakness, skin rash, swollen lymph glands, neck stiffness, tremors, and convulsions. The virus may also result in paralysis. An article on the WebMD website cautions that, "In some cases, especially in the elderly, the virus may lead to a serious condition called encephalitis, in which the brain becomes inflamed and swollen."

The terror that accompanies the disease was demonstrated in a July 2000 story in the New York *Daily News*. "New Yorkers braced for another summer of fear yesterday after scientists found preliminary evidence that mosquitoes in Westchester and Suffolk counties are carrying the potentially lethal West Nile virus."

Despite assurances by Mayor Giuliani that an outbreak was not imminent, the fear New Yorkers felt was heightened when a bird infected with the virus was found on Staten Island—within the limits of the city itself—prompting ground spraying of pesticides.

During the 1999 WNV epidemic, the disease may have infected as many as 13,000 New Yorkers. The WebMD article advises us that, "Though anyone can be infected, there are certain populations that are at higher risk of developing severe illness. These include people over the age of 50 and anyone with an illness or on medication that suppresses the immune system (for example, people with HIV or kidney failure and people who have had organ transplants)."

The Centers for Disease Control predicts that, "… widespread WNV epizootic activity probably will persist and expand in the United States, larger outbreaks of WNV infection and human illness are possible if adequate surveillance, prevention activities, and mosquito control are not established and maintained."

Despite the fact that several drug companies are now testing medicinal cures for West Nile Virus, so far no effective vaccine has been discovered, and researchers are unwilling to predict when one will finally be developed. Although relatively few people will ever contract WNV—and fewer still develop severe or fatal symptoms—the outbreak in Louisiana in the summer of 2002 may be an ominous sign that the disease is becoming more widespread in the United States.

One of the most virulent mosquito-borne viruses is encephalitis, an acute inflammation of the brain. Besides WNV, the primary strains of the disease are St. Louis Encephalitis, Japanese Encephalitis, and equine encephalitis. An article on the Mayo Clinic website describes the symptoms of encephalitis as: "Drowsiness, confusion and disorientation, seizures, sudden fever, severe headache, nausea and vomiting, tremors, and bulging in the soft spots (fontanelles) of the skull in infants, and, stiff neck—occasionally."

According to a fact sheet from Ohio State University, "Encephalitis can infect humans, horses, and a variety of other mammals and birds. Eastern equine encephalomyelitis (EEE), although very rare is frequently fatal …. Transmission of the disease occurs when an infected mosquito takes a blood meal. Birds serve as natural hosts for EEE and St. Louis encephalitis (SLE). St. Louis encephalitis, like EEE is an epidemic disease, meaning that it is usually rare. It can be absent from an area for several years and then reoccur suddenly without warning."

Yet another mosquito-borne disease is yellow fever. The Centers for Disease Control describes yellow fever as, "… a viral disease found in parts of Africa and South America. It is transmitted to humans by a mosquito bite."

The New York State Department of Health adds that, "The disease can affect both sexes, all ages and races. Jungle yellow fever, of Central and South America, occurs predominantly among adult males 20 to 40 years old who are exposed in the tropical forests. Initial symptoms may be dengue-like and include fever, headache, vomiting and backache. As the disease progresses, the pulse slows and weakens, and bleeding of the gums and bloody urine occur. Jaundice may also occur. Symptoms occur within three to six days after exposure. There is no specific treatment for yellow fever. People traveling to areas where yellow fever may exist should be immunized."

There is one mosquito-borne virus that doesn't threaten humans but can be fatal to our pets. The disease is dog-heartworm (the virus also strikes cats). An article on the Dog Owners Guide website has this to say about the virus: "Once considered a parasite of southern climates, the Heartworm (Dirofilaria immitis) is now recognized as a major global pest affecting dogs, wolves, coyotes, and foxes. The worms grow and multiply, infesting the chambers on the right side of the heart and the arteries in the lungs. They can also lodge in the veins of the liver and the veins entering the heart."

You might not realize that your pet is infested with Heartworm for up to a year after the animal initially contracts the virus. The first sign of the disease is usually a cough, which steadily worsens. The dog then becomes listless and weak—sometimes to the point of fainting—loses weight, and may cough up blood. Congestive heart failure often follows, and at this point many animals simply cannot be saved.

While mosquitoes carry diseases that can debilitate or kill humans, another insect—locusts—can inflict widespread suffering in quite a different way. Locusts devour our food in the fields, often leaving so little wheat, barley, beans, corn, and other crops that in the Third World, tens of thousands of people have starved to death in the months following a locust invasion. An article on the Disaster Relief website carries this dire assessment by the Food and Agriculture Organization of the United Nations (FAO): "During a plague or invasion of desert locusts, the bugs can spread over millions of square miles or as many as 60 countries. They pose a threat because they eat so much; during an invasion, *they can eat enough to threaten the food supply for one-tenth of the world's population.*" (Italics added.)

A PLAGUE OVER THE LAND

Locusts have plagued humans for millennia. Shortly after humans first began to farm around 8000 B.C.E. in the Fertile Crescent of ancient Mesopotamia—today the countries of Iraq, Turkey, Syria, and Jordan—the first locusts appeared to devastate the harvest. In ancient times, the insects commonly fed on fields of wheat, edible seeds, barley, and similar crops. Today, locusts will eat most green crops—especially vegetables—as well as a host of wild vegetation. They can also devastate pastures, lawns, flowers, and fruit trees. They have even been known to damage urban parks and sports stadiums.

Perhaps the most well-known locust invasion in the United States occurred in Utah in 1848. Shortly after Mormon settlers began farming near Salt Lake City, a huge swarm of horned locusts descended on their fields. Just when all seemed lost and starvation loomed, several flocks of California gulls arrived and ate all the insects. The Mormons were so grateful that they erected a monument in the gulls' honor.

When locusts begin to migrate, their swarms can consist of billions of insects, and their massed bodies will actually block out the sun. According to an article on the Nature website, "The largest swarm ever recorded *contained an estimated 12.5 trillion locusts. It covered several hundred square miles* [italics added]. Such swarms are so big that they are easily tracked by radar."

Locusts average about two inches in length. They have a head, thorax, and abdomen, six feet, four wings, and a stiff outer shell called an exoskeleton. For reasons not yet understood, locusts have five eyes: two large compound eyes that can see in all directions, and three smaller eyes.

The insects can be found in every region of the world except the Arctic and Antarctic. Locusts have two behavioral states: the solitary phase and the gregarious phase. While normally solitary, when the insects experience overcrowding, a scarcity of food, or an unfavorable habitat, they will go through a phase change. The locusts first become agitated, and then gather in large swarms and take to the skies. Swarms have been known to cross oceans, riding the wind from one continent to another. Frequently, an area that has been free of locusts for decades or longer will suddenly suffer an infestation of the voracious insects when the wind brings in a huge swarm. In recent years, swarms of locusts have devoured crops in Asia, the Middle East, the former Soviet Union, Africa, and North America. Close to home, a plague of the insects devoured tens of thousands of acres of crops in southeast Mexico in 1999. The locusts did the most damage to fields of corn, beans, and sorghum.

An article carried by the Reuters News Service quoted Sergio Constance, local delegate from the federal agriculture ministry: "… The insects have an average length of six inches and fly in columns several miles long. The size of the clouds [of locusts] is astonishing. They are at least two kilometers (1.25 miles) and we have had reports of up to eight kilometers (five miles)."

Although huge swarms of locusts already threaten to bring starvation to tens of millions of people in the Third World, the plague could quickly spread and intensify if the greenhouse effect continues to warm the planet. A rise of only a couple of degrees Fahrenheit could allow the insects to fly across the Mediterranean from Africa and devour the olive groves of Italy and the vineyards of France. Swarms could wipe out the wheat fields of the Ukraine and the ornamental gardens of Japan.

The United States is far from immune to the threat. Immense swarms of locusts are already in Mexico. String a couple of warmer-than-usual summers together and the bugs will cross the border by the billions, eating their way north from Texas into our country's breadbasket.

Envision yourself for a moment as a wheat farmer in Kansas. Your fields are almost ready to harvest, the tall stalks swaying in the gentle prairie wind. Then one morning, the sky suddenly darkens and an ominous still falls over your farm. You look up and your blood turns cold. There, flying in fast from the south, is the largest swarm of locusts you have ever seen. There must be billions of them! You know what's coming, but there's nothing you can do. Your entire crop—a year's hard work—is about to disappear down the gullet of insects no bigger than your little finger. Your wife runs out of the house and stands beside you, tears streaming down her cheeks. Neither of you utter a word. What is there to say? You are confronted with a force of nature too powerful for you to battle. As you watch in shock and horror, the locusts descend on your fields and begin to eat. Within hours, there is not a head of wheat left on your farm. With no crop to sell, you won't have the money to pay your bills, meet the bank loan, or buy seed to plant next spring. You face ruin, brought to your knees by a bug.

If temperatures continue to rise, such scenarios will play out all over America—indeed, all over the world.

CHAPTER 9: INSECT INVASIONS

If the nations of the world do not join in a united effort to stop polluting the atmosphere—and there is little evidence that they will—the greenhouse effect will worsen, and insect populations will explode as the earth continues to warm. In all likelihood, in the years ahead, populations of killer bees, ants, mosquitoes, and locusts will increase 10- or 100- or 1,000-fold. More and more people will die of stings and starvation. The ground will crawl and the air will be choked with insects. Humanity's reign as the supreme species on Earth will be challenged, and perhaps even end.

BIOENGINEERING BLUNDERS

Like many highflying biotech ventures, the BioGard Advanced Solutions NA (North America) Corporation was initially designed to pull a big IPO pop, sell a mass of overvalued stock to gullible investors, and make the company founders fabulously rich when they cashed in their stock options and got out before the roof fell in. But BioGard came late to the game, and the big stock pops were temporarily no more, due to a demoralized Wall Street in the throes of a big hangover from the previous get-rich-quick period.

The result was that the company actually had to do some real business to keep itself and its owners afloat. Headquarters were located in suburban Connecticut near the New York border, conveniently close to Manhattan. A company founder had gone to prep school with a man who was now an important official in the administration in Washington, D.C.

This "old boy" contact led to BioGard's receiving a lucrative government contract to develop a biogenetically engineered anti-drug fungus. Washington's drug enforcement machinery was seeking bio approaches to the war on drugs. Simply put, most major illicit drugs in the western hemisphere were the product of plants: marijuana, opiate-producing poppies, and the coca leaf. Previous eradication efforts had failed due to the human factor: Namely, too many interested parties had a financial stake in subverting the drug war and seeing that the crops were not wiped out.

Government planners proposed using genetically altered plants and fungi to attack and destroy the narcotic plants in their own ecosystems. It was a different type of biological warfare, made possible by advances in gene-splicing that allowed for the creation of unique—and profitably patentable—life forms.

The biogeneticists at BioGard approached the problem by modifying the DNA of a fungus, splicing gene segments from related donors, and recombining them into a new and self-reproducing life form according to the dictates and specifications of the client. The solution was a fungus that attacked narcotic plants, attaching to them and feeding off them until the host plant died, whereupon the fungi would sporulate, releasing clouds of microscopic spores that would attach themselves to other narcotic plants and resume the process. The cycle would end when the last narcotic plant in the region was consumed.

CHAPTER 10: BIOENGINEERING BLUNDERS

The fungi could be bioengineered to selectively attack opiates, cannabinoids, or cocaine alkoloids. Bioengineering also ensured that the fungi would attack only the targeted criminal plant and no others. That was the theory.

At the same time, financial reverses resulted in cutbacks that decimated the BioGard research staff. Remaining staffers were demoralized. The best found positions somewhere else, while the B-team stayed on. That didn't worry the company owners. The real work had already been done, resulting in the creation of the patented narcophagic fungi strains. All that remained was the fine-tuning, and even the uninspired slackers left in the labs couldn't botch that job too badly. That was the theory.

One ordinary workday, a lab technician went out for a long liquid lunch. He knew he was drinking too much, but what did he care? BioGard would be bankrupt in a month. Securities and Exchange Commission investigators were probing the company, whose treasury had been looted by the company's long-gone top officers.

Returning to work that afternoon, the technician was loose, sloppy. He left his lab coat in his locker. Working alone, he dropped a beaker, scattering glass shards and water around the supposedly sterile environment. Finally wrapping it up for the day, he inadvertently released fungi spores from an improperly sealed containment chamber. The laboratory should have been safe from even the worst bumblings of a drunken employee, with safeguard upon safeguard—but properly guarding against contamination is expensive, requiring all kinds of airlocks, hermetically sealed chambers, sensors, scrubbers, and decontaminants. Not cost-effective, decreed the company owners, who opted not to acquire the equipment. With minimal protective safeguards, an accident was only a matter of time.

Covered with countless invisible fungal spores, the woozy lab tech left the facility, crossed the parking lot, got in his car, and began weaving his way home—with all the windows down.

That was how the bioengineered fungi entered the world. The lab tech shed spores everywhere, spilling a trail of them from the lab to his car and beyond, leaving a swirling wake of them in the world beyond the site's chain-link fences and sleepily guarded gate.

Now loose in the ecosystem, of the countless millions of genetically altered spores released, the majority perished for lack of any narcotic-producing plants to prey upon. But a sizeable minority proved to be more adaptable, attaching themselves to the nearest green plants and thriving quite nicely, even without any narcotic material present in the plants.

To these less-discriminating gourmands, any plant would do: a blade of grass, a flowering blossom, a tree leaf. As the spores germinated, the fungi swiftly progressed from blades of grass to entire lawns, from single leaves to the trees that bore them, from single flowers to expansive gardens.

Within a few months, the fungi had eaten its way through the plant material of a wide swathe of southern Connecticut, as well as much of Westchester County in New York—and the population was suddenly taking notice. Forests were graveyards of dead, bare trees. Former lawns and parklands were expanses of brown dirt, with no blade of grass to be seen. The greatest eco-crisis in history was off and running. Each puff of wind spread the increasingly versatile spores to the four corners of the world, all of which would eventually become denuded of green growing things if the plant-destroying fungi were not itself destroyed.

As the green perished, so, too, would perish most of the animals inhabiting the earth, including the upright primate with opposable thumbs and diabolical ingenuity, Homo sapiens.

———————————————■———————————————

As the third millennium dawns, bioengineers are creating weird new life forms that fly in the face of genetic structures that have existed for millions of years. Among them are a "master race" of microbes with increased powers to infect humans and wildlife; "Terminator" trees that will likely wipe out insects, birds, and mammals; "Frankenfoods" that threaten both human health and the environment; and robots with the transplanted brains of fishes.

In a genetic breakthrough that is at once exhilarating and foreboding, scientists have created the first synthetic DNA, the molecules that form the blueprint for life. "The breakthrough means that the first artificial organisms could be 'born' within two years," reads a 2000 story in British Columbia's *Victoria Times Colonist*.

Scientists at the University of Texas synthesized the DNA, which will be used to create the world's first man-made organism. If the new life form can feed and reproduce, the breakthrough experiment will be considered a stunning success by proponents of the work.

However, many researchers consider the creation of new life forms a direct threat to both human health and the environment. They point out that there is no way we can be certain of the consequences of creating genetically altered organisms, and insist that there should be more public debate before man assumes the role of nature.

One has only to remember the murderous monster that Frankenstein created when he attempted to "play God"—or read the accounts of bioengineering blunders that follow—to get an uneasy feeling that Mr. Juniper may be right. Do humans have the right to tamper with the natural genetic makeup of animals and plants? It is not just a question of morals and ethics, but perhaps a question of the very survival of humans as well.

Creating new species became a very real possibility when scientists announced that they had completed a "working draft" of the human genome in 2000. A *New York Times* article defines the human genome as "the chemical code needed to build a human being. The blueprint comprises DNA (dioxyribonucleic acid), a long molecular chain of phosphate and sugar in the shape of a double-helix ladder connected by rungs called bases. Each person's DNA is unique, except in the case of identical twins."

> Do humans have the right to tamper with the natural genetic makeup of animals and plants?

A MAP TO THE GENETIC FUTURE

Geneticists believe that the mapping of the human genome is an incredible breakthrough that will enable scientists to remedy birth defects, build defenses against diseases, and even grow replacement organs, skin, and limbs. Others view the development with alarm.

In a press release from the Indigenous Peoples Council on Biocolonialism, Debra Harry, a descendant of the Northern Paiute Indian tribe of western Nevada and Executive Director of the Council, said, "This announcement, and genetic research generally, raises serious issues of concern to indigenous peoples. Now that the sequencing project is complete more scientists will turn their attention to human genetic diversity, which includes the collection and study of the DNA of indigenous peoples, and possible manipulations of their DNA, which violate the natural genetic integrity of their ancestry.'"

Is Ms. Harry crying wolf? Hardly. Patents have actually been filed on the DNA of indigenous people from Panama and the Solomon Islands. Although the applications were later relinquished, the U.S. Patent and Trademarks Office did approve another patent on the cell line of a native of New Guinea. The patent applicant was the U.S. Department of Health and Human Services and the National Institutes of Health (NIH). Although the NIH did not pursue the patent, the cell line is now available to genetic researchers worldwide.

Science is the revelation of nature, but does that mean exploitation as well? How would you like to have your genes—your most vital heritage to your children, your grandchildren, and all your line that follow—for sale? Could scientists use your genes to clone you? Could there be 10,000 replicas of you in different parts of the world? Slaves of science who will never see the outside of a laboratory?

The Council on Biocolonialism press release goes on to recount this horror story. Donna Gardiner, a Maori [the indigenous people of New Zealand] researcher, has written extensively on the activities of Selbourne Biological Services, a biotech corporation operating in New Zealand. Referring to Selbourne's importation of human DNA for insertion into sheep, an outraged Gardiner expressed her view that, "The thought of human and animal genes being mixed [is] totally abhorrent and offensive both culturally and morally."

This all-but-unbelievable incident highlights the potential for human genetic manipulation when mechanisms for oversight, control, and accountability are lacking. "Although the New Zealand DNA project was undoubtedly designed to engender new traits in the sheep, other scientists are researching ways to create entirely new species, including creatures that are part human and part animal.

A New York scientist, Stuart A. Newman, has applied for a patent on a technique in which human embryo cells would be combined with the embryo cells of an ape or other nonhuman primate. The cells of the two species would fuse into a single embryo that would then be implanted in the womb of either a woman or an ape. Newman proposes to call the half-human-half-ape a "chimera," after the beast of Greek mythology that had a lion's head, a goat's body, and a serpent's tail. Although Newman says he never intends to create such creatures and he only applied for the patent to spark debate about the morality of bioengineering humans, who is to say that other scientists are not exploring ways to create hybrid humans? After all, we are already transferring human genes to animals to create everything from vaccines to mother's milk.

In a *Washington Post* article, correspondent Rick Weiss quotes the concerns of Thomas Murray, director of the Center for Biomedical Ethics at Case Western Reserve University. "'It is a classic slippery slope,'" Murray said. "'If we put one human gene in an animal, or two or three, some people may get nervous, but you're clearly not making a person yet. But when you talk about a hefty percentage of the cells being human ... this really is problematic. Then you have to ask these very hard questions about what it means to be human.'"

Most of us have a very clear idea of what it means to be human—although there are murderers, torturers, and other evil beings among us who might fairly be considered beasts. Yet, in this age of bioengineering, the boundary between Homo sapiens and other animals seems to be increasingly blurred for geneticists and researchers.

Another area of bioengineering—the so-called "Frankenstein technology"—is also sparking sharp debate among scientists and ethicists. The experimental science—already approved for use in Great Britain—enables geneticists to clone cells from embryos and use them to grow new tissue for medical use.

A story in the *London Observer* by correspondents Kamal Ahmed and Gaby Hinsliff reported that the "decision (to permit cloning from embryos) will allow British scientists to take a world lead in cloning research. By taking cells from the embryos, scientists will not only be able to grow new brain tissue to replace damaged material, but also new skin for grafts for burn victims and, ultimately, new organs such as hearts, kidneys, and livers."

Although, theoretically, cloning would also allow people to establish their own "tissue bank"—a form of genetic insurance against future debilitating diseases—the process of cloning from an embryo or from ourselves raises a fiercely debated moral dilemma. Are we creating living organisms for our own use rather than for whatever purposes nature—many would say God—intends?

IF YOU CAN TAMPER WITH THE ANIMALS ...

Even though the genetic modification of animal species other than humans is far less controversial, it can be equally disquieting. We are, after all, tampering with genetic structures that evolved over millions of years. How can we be sure that—in the process of redesigning nature—we are not creating artificial life forms as unpredictable and potentially hostile as aliens from another planet?

Indeed, some of the bioengineering experiments carried out in recent years could only be called "otherworldly." For instance—for reasons known only to themselves—French genetic researchers have used the genes of a jellyfish to create a rabbit named Alba that glows green when placed under an ultraviolet light. In an article for ABC News, correspondent Amanda Onion reported, "Alba appears like any other furry white rabbit. But place her under a black light, and her eyes, whiskers and fur glow an otherworldly green."

The French scientists created Alba using a process called zygote microinjection. While the technology has some practical uses—tracing the effects of a new drug as it travels through the body and expediting tumor removal by making cancer cells glow green are two—it has also drawn strong disapproval from animal-rights activists, who view the experimentation as simply the newest form of cruelty to animals.

Moving from the silly to the weird, the Associated Press reports from Plattsburgh, New York, that a company called Nexia Biotechnologies has been doing truly strange things with goats. "The goats have been bred with a spider gene so their milk provides a unique protein. The company then plans to extract the protein from the milk to produce fibers—called Biosteel—for bulletproof vests, aerospace and medical supplies. Spider silk has a unique combination of strength and elasticity with an ultra-lightweight fiber. In January, Nexia announced the birth of two bio-steel goats."

Not to be outdone by goat-spiders, a biotechnology company called PPL Therapeutics has discovered a novel way to produce infant formula. John von Radowitz, medical correspondent for *PA News*, reports, "Genetic scientists are working toward creating cows which produce human breast milk. Already a 20-strong herd exists whose milk contains a protein component of human milk. ... Ultimately the scientists hope to 'knock out' genes producing animal protein in cow's milk while elevating the levels of human protein. The result would be a cow whose milk is virtually the same as that from a human mother's breast."

How about a lobster that belongs in a sci-fi movie? A story in the Ottawa Citizen reports, "They should call it Claws. Geneticists are creating the world's biggest lobster after discovering how to block the genes that limit animals' natural growth. In secret laboratory experiments, they have also applied the technique to make giant chickens, sheep and pigs and are attempting to do the same with cattle."

Can you imagine buying a lobster at the local fish store and on the way home it eats the back seat? How about having chickens the size of condors wandering around your barnyard, or trying to round up cattle that are as big as dump trucks?

Scientists are also developing monster fish. In an article for the Environmental News Network, Jean-Michel Cousteau writes, "Behold the 'superfish,' a salmon that grows six times as fast and twice as large as normal farmed Atlantic salmon but only consumes three-quarters as much feed before it is brought to market."

In theory, the superfish is a very positive genetic breakthrough by scientists. As the population of the world continues to mushroom, more and more food will be needed. Yet, as so often happens when humans tinker with nature, the creation of the superfish may have unexpected side effects. Research on the introduction of genetically altered species into the wild has shown that up to a third of the new life forms don't reach sexual maturity. This means that the population will inevitably decrease, and eventually go extinct.

As strange as genetically modified superfish may seem, scientists have developed an even weirder "artificial animal"—a hybrid creature with a mechanical body controlled by the brain of a fish. This cyborg, chimera, or whatever you want to call it, was developed by Ferdinando Mussa-Ivaldi of Northwestern University and his colleagues at the University of Illinois and the University of Genoa, Italy. They combined the brainstem and part of the spinal cord of a lamprey, a primitive eel-like vertebrate, with a commercially available two-wheeled robot module called a Khepera.

As an article in *New Scientist* magazine by Duncan Graham-Rowe reveals, "Light sensors housed in the mechanical body feed the brain sensory information. The brain tissue processes this information to generate command signals which tell the robot's motors which way to turn in response to its environment. ... When the robot was presented with a number of light stimuli, its lamprey brain responded with a variety of behaviors, such as following the light, avoiding the light and moving in circles."

Fish-brained robots leave you cold? Perhaps you'd be more interested in killer trees? In a story in *London's Daily Telegraph*, correspondents Oliver Tickell and Charles Clover reported, "'Terminator' trees, genetically engineered never to flower, could ensure a silent spring in the forests of the future. Such trees will grow faster than before, but will be devoid of the bees, butterflies, moths, birds and squirrels which depend on pollen, seed and nectar, scientists said."

Although the geneticists plan to make the fast-growing trees sterile so that they cannot contaminate wild species with modified DNA, there is really no guarantee that one or more of the bioengineered trees won't remain able to pollinate and thus crossbreed with trees growing naturally in nearby forests.

Environmental correspondent Paul Brown filed an alarming story on super-trees in London's *Guardian* newspaper. "Environmentalists yesterday warned of the dangers of genetically modified super-trees which can cross pollinate with native trees over a distance of 400 miles and which are being grown in field trials without knowledge of the consequences."

One has only to look at the history of genetically modified crops to get extremely nervous at the prospect of super-trees. For several years, scientists have been worried that the use of herbicide-tolerant canola—a plant that produces seeds rich in oil—would result in cross-pollination with other plants. The fear was that if bees or the wind spread pollen from the genetically modified canola to areas beyond the control fields, super-resistant weeds could develop.

A 2000 story in the *Globe and Mail*, Canada's major national newspaper, reported that canola varieties resistant to Roundup, Liberty, Pursuit, and Odyessy (all herbicides) have been sold in Canada for some time, and now, "herbicide-resistant plants are spreading like wildfire."

If farmers can't kill weeds with herbicides, they'll be forced to spend more time, energy, and money ridding their fields of unwanted plant intruders. In a worst-case scenario, the new super-weeds could threaten entire crops. Cross-pollination wasn't supposed to happen, but it did, and it furnished yet another example of the myriad things that can go wrong with biotech experiments. Soya-bean farmers are all too familiar with the problem. Monsanto, the same agribiotech giant that developed herbicide-resistant canola, also bioengineered herbicide-resistant soya beans. A great idea, until Georgia and adjacent southern states experienced the two hottest springs since the beans were launched in 1996. Farmers noticed that the genetically modified soya beans were smaller than naturally grown beans and their yields were less. Worse still, the stems of the bioengineered beans were splitting open, causing catastrophic crop losses. The promised quantum leap forward in agriculture had turned into a nightmare.

More and more eminent scientists are speaking out against bioengineered plants and animals. Professor Richard Lacey, a microbiologist, medical doctor, and professor of Food Safety at England's Leeds University, believes that genetically modified meat, fish, and vegetables pose unlimited health risks to humans. "The fact is, it is virtually impossible to even conceive of a testing procedure to assess the health effects of genetically engineered foods when introduced into the food chain," he says, "nor is there any valid nutritional or public interest reason for their introduction."

Only future generations will be able to decide whether the terrible risk of bioengineering new species of plants and animals is ultimately worth taking.

EPILOGUE

Like everything in life, when it comes to the doomsday scenarios presented in this book, there are some things we can control and some things we cannot.

We can try to do something about the worsening greenhouse effect, cyberterrorism, looming plagues, bioengineering blunders, and the proliferation of weapons of mass destruction. Yet any effort we make to forestall or eliminate one or more of these threats will require that we as humans undergo a very fundamental transformation in our way of looking at the world and at each other.

We shall have to put aside the greed, arrogance toward nature, and cultural, religious, and racial hatreds that have brought us to the brink of catastrophe. Throughout the entire history of humankind, we have not been able to conquer these demons. Can we do it now—even if not doing so might well mean the extinction of our species? History and reason tell us probably not. In all likelihood, we shall doom ourselves.

As to the extinction scenarios that are not in our hands—asteroid impacts, massive volcanic eruptions, the coming ice age, mega-tsunamis, and insect invasions—there is simply nothing we can do to alter the inevitable. We may think we can use our mighty technological prowess to save our species—nuclear weapons to destroy incoming asteroids, giant dams to divert warm ocean currents and melt advancing ice sheets—but in the end all our efforts will be futile, for it is nature, not man, that reigns supreme on Earth.

At some point in the future—and no one knows when—one of the doomsday scenarios described in this book *will* occur, and the human species will cease to exist. When an asteroid impact wiped out the dinosaurs, we replaced the huge reptiles as the dominant species. When we, in turn, vanish, some other life form will take our place, and this cycle will continue for the next five or six billion years—the projected remaining life span of the sun.

Perhaps, in the final analysis, we should not worry about tomorrow—for tomorrow will be what tomorrow will be—but rather seize each day we are given. Love our families, cherish our friends, and forgive our enemies, open our eyes to the beauty of nature around us. Before it's too late, we need to stop and smell the roses, for roses—like the human species—cannot bloom forever.

INDEX

A

acetylcholine, 7

act of war (*casus belli*), 4

active volcanoes, 47

Adams, Jonathan, 72

Aedes aegypti, 123

aeromagnetic data, 51

Afghanistan, Taliban regime, 3
> Osama bin Laden, 14

Africanized honey bees (killer bees), 159-162

Agassiz's theory, geological evidence of ancient ice ages, 80

AIDS, HIV (Human Immunodeficiency Virus), 117-119

airports
> McCarran International Airport (Las Vegas), Africanized honey bees invasion, 161
>
> O'Hare Airport (Chicago), cyberterrorism, 137
>
> Ronald Reagan Airport (Washington, D.C.), cyberterrorism, 137

al Qaeda, nuclear weapons threat, 14
> Osama bin Laden, 14

Alba (genetically engineered rabbit), bioengineering, 188

Alexander, Yonah, 146

Alfred P. Murrah Federal Building, 16
> McVeigh, Timothy, 16

Alvarez, Luis, evidence of mass extinction of dinosaurs by an asteroid, 30-32

Alvarez, Walter, evidence of mass extinction of dinosaurs by an asteroid, 30-32

Animals of the Rainforest, 164

anonymity of cyberterrorists, 140

Antarctica, subglacial volcanism, Mount Erebus, 51

anthrax (biological agent), 8, 132
> Gruinard Island research, 12-13

ants, 162
> army, 162-166
>> clamping power of the mandibles, 164
>>
>> nests (bivouacs), 163
>
> fire, 166-170

Army Ant web page (Zach Fulton), 164

Asahara, Shoko, 10

asteroids, 22
> Catalina Sky Survey, 26
>
> detection and defense, 29
>
> Earth transformations, 25
>
> extinctions, 30
>> Devonian period, 30
>>
>> dinosaurs, 32
>>
>> K-T extinction, 30-32
>>
>> Ordovician period, 30
>>
>> Permian period, 30
>>
>> Triassic period, 30
>
> impact with an ocean, resulting mega-tsunamis, 107-108
>
> LINEAR search program, 26
>
> LONEOS, 26
>
> Lowell Observatory, 23
>
> NEAT program, 26

B

F

G

H

N

INDEX